Build Your Own Secure Linux Blockchain Node

A Complete Guide to Cryptocurrency, Social Media, Content Distribution, and Decentralized Finance

Written by, Lynne Kolestar

Table of Contents

Introduction

Why Blockchain?

Blockchain technology has become one of the most groundbreaking innovations of the 21st century, transforming the way we store, verify, and share information. At its core, blockchain is a decentralized system, meaning it doesn't rely on a central authority—such as a bank, government, or tech company—to manage data. Instead, it uses a network of computers—sometimes local, sometimes remote—all synced together through secure software to ensure that information is protected, transparent, and unchangeable. This technology has gained significant attention because it overcomes the limitations of traditional, centralized systems. But what exactly makes blockchain so important, and why is it generating so much interest?

The Rise of Decentralized Technologies

For decades, the internet has been built on centralized technologies, where large corporations control vast amounts of data, financial systems, and services. These central authorities bear the significant costs of equipment and operations, and users must often trust them to manage their personal information and transactions. This reliance can lead to issues such as security breaches, privacy violations, and inefficiencies.

Blockchain, however, offers an alternative: decentralization. Instead of relying on a single organization or entity to control and validate transactions, blockchain distributes this responsibility across a network of nodes, making it far more secure and resistant to censorship, fraud, or manipulation. With decentralized technologies, data is stored in multiple locations, and any changes made to the ledger require consensus from the network, ensuring that all participants have an equal say. This creates a trustless environment, where participants do not need to trust a central entity, only the rules encoded into the blockchain itself.

As a result, decentralized technologies, including blockchain, have sparked a wave of innovation across various sectors, from finance to entertainment and beyond. This shift toward decentralization is seen as a fundamental change in how we interact with digital services and data. By eliminating intermediaries and providing more control to users, blockchain technologies empower individuals and organizations alike to manage their assets, identities, and data with greater autonomy.

Benefits of Owning and Running Your Own Blockchain Node

One of the most compelling reasons to learn about blockchain is the opportunity to pursue your own interests at a low cost, whether through experimentation or by supporting an existing digital infrastructure. By running your own blockchain node, you become an integral part of the decentralized network, contributing to its integrity and security.

Some key benefits of running your own blockchain node:

Security and Privacy: Running your own node provides you with more control over your data and ensures that your transactions are validated directly by you. This minimizes the risk of third-party interference or data breaches, providing a more secure and private way to interact with the blockchain.

Network Participation: By running a node, you contribute to the decentralization of the blockchain network. You help validate transactions, create blocks, and maintain the integrity of the network. This level of participation not only enhances the security and efficiency of the network but also strengthens the entire blockchain ecosystem.

Transparency and Trust: Running a node gives you direct access to the blockchain's data, allowing you to independently verify transactions and blocks. This transparency builds trust in the system since you don't have to rely on any third parties to provide accurate information.

It allows you to see exactly how the network operates and ensures that no one is manipulating or censoring data.

Earn Rewards (in Some Cases): Depending on the blockchain network you are running, there may be rewards for your participation. For example, if you're running a cryptocurrency node, you may earn cryptocurrency rewards for verifying transactions or contributing to the network's operation (such as through staking in Proof-of-Stake systems or mining in Proof-of-Work systems).

Independence from Centralized Platforms: Running your own blockchain node provides you with greater autonomy over your interactions with the network. Unlike centralized services that rely on third-party intermediaries, you can transact and interact directly with the blockchain, without needing to trust an external entity. This makes your digital activities more resilient to censorship, outages, and vulnerabilities associated with centralized services.

Owning and operating your own blockchain node empowers you to take control of your digital activities, whether you're using blockchain for cryptocurrency, personal data management, or other decentralized applications. It provides the foundation for a more secure, private, and trustworthy digital future.

Overview of Use Cases: Cryptocurrency, Social Media, Content Distribution, and Decentralized Finance

While blockchain is best known for its role in the world of cryptocurrency, the technology's applications extend far beyond digital currencies. It's increasingly being used for everything from social media and content distribution to transforming traditional financial systems and improving the efficiency and security of the medical industry.

Below is an overview of the most prominent use cases for blockchain technology:

Cryptocurrency: The most popular and widely known application of blockchain technology is in cryptocurrencies like Bitcoin, Ethereum, and many others. Cryptocurrency uses blockchain to enable decentralized, peer-to-peer transactions without relying on traditional financial institutions. By validating and recording transactions on a blockchain, cryptocurrencies offer an alternative to centralized banking systems, providing more privacy, lower transaction fees, and faster transfers across borders.

Social Media: Traditional social media platforms are centralized, meaning a single company controls both the data and interactions between users. Blockchain can help decentralize social media, giving users ownership of their content and more control over their data. Platforms like Steemit, and Hive are examples of blockchain-based social media, where users can earn tokens for creating and sharing content, promoting a more equitable distribution of value.

Content Distribution: The digital content industry is rife with inefficiencies and unfair distribution of revenue. Blockchain can address these issues by providing a decentralized method of distributing content. Platforms like Audius, for example, use blockchain to enable musicians and content creators to directly share their work with audiences, cutting out middlemen such as record labels or streaming services. This not only improves revenue for creators but also gives users more direct access to content. In the realm of science, ResearchHub and DataBroker DAO use blockchain to encourage the sharing of research data and make scientific findings more accessible and transparent. In education, Uphold and Disciplina are blockchain-based platforms that enable secure, verifiable academic credentials, reducing fraud. Meanwhile, in the arts, platforms like Async Art and SuperRare empower digital artists by allowing them to tokenize their work as NFTs, ensuring authenticity and enabling direct transactions with collectors.

Decentralized Finance (DeFi): Decentralized finance (DeFi) is an umbrella term for financial services built on blockchain technology. It encompasses everything from lending and borrowing to decentralized exchanges (DEXs) and stablecoins. DeFi platforms run on smart contracts—self-executing contracts with terms directly written into code—which eliminates the need for intermediaries like banks or financial institutions. DeFi represents a transformative shift in how financial systems are structured, offering increased accessibility, lower costs, and greater transparency.

As can be noted, blockchain's potential extends far beyond cryptocurrency. It has the ability to disrupt entire industries by decentralizing and democratizing systems, providing individuals and communities with more control, privacy, and opportunities. Running a blockchain node opens up a world of possibilities, not only in cryptocurrency but in a wide array of sectors, each of which could benefit from the inherent advantages of blockchain technology.

What You Will Learn

This book is designed not only to introduce Linux-based blockchain technologies to novices, intermediate users, and experienced practitioners, but also to equip you with the skills and knowledge needed to effectively set up, secure, and optimize a Linux server for running blockchain

Setting Up a Secure Linux Server

You will learn how to:

Install and configure a Linux server: You'll be guided through the installation of a minimal Linux distribution suitable for blockchain node operations, such as Debian/Ubuntu or CentOS. This will also include selecting the right server environment (cloud-based, VPS, or physical server).

Harden your server: Security is a critical aspect of running blockchain nodes. You will understand best practices for configuring a firewall, setting up secure access via SSH, enabling automatic updates, and ensuring your server is not vulnerable to common attacks.

Secure remote access: You will learn how to set up SSH keys for secure and passwordless login, disable unnecessary services, and configure multi-factor authentication (MFA) for extra security.

Installing and Running Blockchain Nodes for Multiple Applications

You will be introduced to the process of:

Installing Blockchain Clients: Depending on your intended use, you will be guided through the installation of popular blockchain clients like Bitcoin Core, Geth (Ethereum), and others. These clients will enable you to interact with and validate the blockchain.

Running Full Nodes and Light Nodes: You will learn the difference between running a full node, which downloads and verifies the entire blockchain to ensure complete network validation, and a light node, which only downloads a subset of the blockchain that is relevant to the user, reducing resource requirements and improving efficiency.

Running multiple nodes on the same server: In scenarios where you need to manage several blockchain applications or networks, you will discover how to run multiple blockchain nodes on a single server. This section covers the use of virtualization, Docker, and other tools to isolate environments for various blockchain networks.

How to Ensure Privacy, Security, and Optimization of Your Node

As blockchain nodes often handle sensitive data, you will gain a solid understanding of:

Privacy considerations: How to ensure that your node operation does not expose you to privacy risks. You will learn about IP anonymization techniques such as VPNs or Tor for hiding your node's IP address.

Security measures: Key techniques to protect your blockchain node from potential attacks such as DDoS, Sybil attacks, and common network vulnerabilities. This includes best practices for securing wallet information and private keys.

Optimizing node performance: Effective methods for improving your node's efficiency, such as optimizing disk usage, adjusting memory allocations, and enhancing blockchain synchronization speeds.

Exploring Real-World Applications of Blockchain Beyond Cryptocurrency

This book also explores how blockchains are used in industries beyond cryptocurrency, such as:

Supply chain management: Blockchain's role in tracking products, ensuring transparency, and verifying authenticity in the supply chain.

Decentralized finance (DeFi): How blockchain is revolutionizing finance through decentralized lending, borrowing, and trading without traditional intermediaries.

Digital identity and voting systems: Exploring how blockchain can be used for secure, verifiable digital identities and transparent voting systems.

Data storage and file sharing: The potential of blockchain for securely storing and sharing large data sets, as demonstrated by projects like Filecoin and IPFS.

Prerequisites

Before diving into the detailed process of setting up your blockchain node, there are a few basic concepts and skills that will help you get the most out of this guide. While not all of these prerequisites are mandatory, having a basic understanding of the following will ensure you are fully prepared.

Basic Understanding of Linux (Helpful but Not Mandatory)

While this guide is designed to be accessible to all users, including those new to Linux, having a basic understanding of Linux commands and concepts will be beneficial. For a deeper understanding of Linux, you may find the other books in my *The Linux Server Mastery Series*, available on Amazon, to be valuable resources.

Specifically, you should familiarize yourself with:

Terminal basics: Knowing how to use the terminal (command line) is essential for interacting with your server.

Basic commands such as ls, cd, pwd, cp, mv, and rm will help you navigate and manipulate files.

Package management: Understanding how to install and manage software on a Linux system using package managers like apt, yum, or dnf will be crucial when installing blockchain clients and dependencies.

For complete beginners, it may be helpful to start with some introductory Linux tutorials or check out my book series, ***The Linux Server Mastery Series***, available on Amazon. But don't worry if you're just starting—this guide will walk you through each step in detail.

Familiarity with Blockchain and Cryptocurrency (Optional but Helpful)

While not strictly required, familiarity with the basic concepts of blockchain and cryptocurrency will help you understand why and how blockchain nodes operate.

Key concepts include:

Blockchain basics: How decentralized ledgers work, how transactions are validated, and what consensus algorithms like Proof of Work (PoW) and Proof of Stake (PoS) are.

Cryptocurrency fundamentals: Understanding how cryptocurrencies like Bitcoin, Ethereum, and others operate on a blockchain, including concepts like wallets, mining, and transactions.

If you are new to blockchain, don't worry—this book will introduce you to the most important concepts and explain how they relate to node operation in a practical way.

Hardware and Software Requirements for Setting Up the Server

For setting up a blockchain server on Linux, you'll need more robust hardware than for basic tasks, but older PCs can still work if they meet certain requirements. Ideally, you should have a multi-core processor like an Intel Core i5/i7 or AMD Ryzen, and at least 8GB of RAM to handle blockchain verification, node syncing, and transaction processing. For storage, a solid-state drive (SSD) with at least 250GB is recommended, as blockchain data grows rapidly and requires fast read/write speeds. A reliable, high-speed internet connection and a 64-bit Linux distribution are also crucial for optimal performance in a blockchain environment.

Before setting up your Linux server and running a blockchain node, you need to ensure your hardware meets the following minimum requirements:

Hardware Requirements:

CPU: A multi-core processor (preferably Intel i5 or better) for optimal performance. Blockchain nodes require processing power, especially for verifying transactions.

Memory: At least 4GB of RAM for basic blockchain applications. More demanding nodes (e.g., Ethereum) may require 8GB or more.

Storage: Depending on the blockchain, disk space requirements can vary significantly. Bitcoin and Ethereum full nodes may require hundreds of gigabytes or even several terabytes of disk space. Ensure you have adequate storage, ideally with an SSD for faster read/write speeds.

Network: A stable, high-speed internet connection is essential, with at least 1Mbps upload/download speed. Blockchain nodes need to sync continuously with the network and communicate with peers.

Software Requirements:

Linux Distribution: Debian/Ubuntu Server or CentOS are commonly recommended distributions for blockchain node setups. The version should be up-to-date to ensure compatibility with the latest software.

Blockchain Client: You'll need to download and install the appropriate blockchain client for the specific network you plan to run. For instance, use Bitcoin Core for Bitcoin, Geth for Ethereum, and similar clients for other blockchains. These clients are available for both Debian/Ubuntu and CentOS Linux distributions, ensuring compatibility with your server setup.

Optional Software: Depending on your use case, you may need additional software like Docker, monitoring tools (e.g., Prometheus, Grafana), or database software for storing blockchain data.

By the end of this book, you will be well-equipped to set up and maintain a secure, efficient blockchain node, explore its real-world applications, and optimize its performance. Whether you are exploring decentralized finance, content distribution, or other blockchain-driven innovations, you'll gain valuable skills to help you leverage the power of decentralized technologies.

Chapter 1: Introduction to Blockchain Technology

What is Blockchain?

Blockchain is the underlying technology behind cryptocurrencies, but its potential extends far beyond digital currencies. At its core, blockchain is a distributed ledger system that securely records transactions across multiple computers in a way that ensures data integrity, privacy, and transparency. The concept is relatively simple but has profound implications for industries ranging from finance to healthcare, social media, and more.

Basic Blockchain Concepts: Blocks, Transactions, and Consensus

To understand blockchain, it's crucial to grasp the basic components that make it work:

Blocks: A block is a container that holds a list of transactions. These blocks are linked together in a chain (hence the name "blockchain"). Each block contains a set of transactions, a timestamp, and a reference (called a "hash") to the previous block. This ensures that the data in the blockchain is unchangeable, as altering one block would require changing all subsequent blocks, which is computationally infeasible.

Transactions: A transaction is a record of an event, such as the transfer of cryptocurrency between two users, or any action that needs to be verified on the blockchain. Transactions are added to blocks and then confirmed by the network. Each transaction typically involves inputs (who is sending the data) and outputs (who is receiving it), along with a digital signature for security and verification.

Consensus: Consensus refers to the process by which blockchain nodes agree on the validity of transactions and the order in which they are added to the blockchain. It ensures that all participants in the network are in sync and that no one can alter the blockchain without detection. Consensus is what makes blockchain a secure, decentralized system.

Types of Blockchain: Public, Private, and Consortium

Blockchain technology comes in several forms, each with its own set of use cases:

Public Blockchains: A public blockchain is open to anyone. Anyone can participate in the network by running a node, validating transactions, and contributing to the consensus process. Bitcoin and Ethereum are prime examples of public blockchains, where anyone can join and participate in the network.

Private Blockchains: In contrast to public blockchains, private blockchains restrict participation to a select group of participants. These are typically used by businesses or organizations to manage internal data or transactions in a secure, private manner. Only authorized parties can access and validate transactions. Examples of private blockchains include Hyperledger Fabric, which is used by businesses for supply chain management and other enterprise solutions, and Ripple (XRP), which is employed by financial institutions for secure, low-cost transactions in a permissioned environment. These blockchains provide greater control, privacy, and security compared to public blockchains.

Consortium Blockchains: A consortium blockchain is a hybrid model where multiple organizations control the blockchain, rather than a single entity. These blockchains are often used by industries or networks that require some degree of centralization but still want to benefit from blockchain's transparency and security. Consortium blockchains are commonly found in industries like banking, supply chain, and healthcare. Examples include R3 Corda, which is widely used in the banking and financial sectors for secure, transparent transactions among multiple financial institutions, and IBM Food Trust, a blockchain platform used by a consortium of companies in the food supply chain to improve transparency, traceability, and efficiency from farm to table. These blockchains enable collaboration between trusted entities while maintaining a level of control and privacy.

Consensus Algorithms: Proof of Work, Proof of Stake, Delegated Proof of Stake

Consensus algorithms are fundamental mechanisms in blockchain technology that ensure all participants within a network agree on the state of the distributed ledger, despite the lack of a central authority. In a blockchain, where data is stored across many nodes, it is crucial to have a way for those nodes to reach a collective agreement about the validity of transactions and the order in which they should be recorded. Without a consensus mechanism, different nodes could have conflicting views of the blockchain, leading to discrepancies or fraud.

Here are some of the most common consensus algorithms:

Proof of Work (PoW): PoW is the consensus algorithm used by Bitcoin and many other cryptocurrencies. In this system, miners—participants in the network—compete to solve complex mathematical puzzles, known as cryptographic challenges, in order to validate transactions and add them to the blockchain. This process requires substantial computational power and energy, which not only ensures the security and integrity of the blockchain but also makes it highly resource-intensive. The difficulty of these puzzles serves as a deterrent to malicious actors, as altering the blockchain would require an impractical amount of computational effort.

Proof of Stake (PoS): Proof of Stake (PoS) is a consensus algorithm in which the likelihood of a participant being chosen to validate a new block and receive a reward is directly proportional to the amount of cryptocurrency they "stake" (or lock up) in the network. In this system, instead of competing to solve energy-intensive puzzles like in Proof of Work, participants (known as validators) are selected to validate blocks based on the number of coins they have committed to the network. The more cryptocurrency a validator stakes, the higher their chances of being chosen to validate the next block, thus earning rewards in the form of transaction fees or newly minted coins. PoS is considered more energy-efficient than Proof of Work because it eliminates the need for miners to perform resource-intensive computations. This not only reduces the environmental impact but also allows for faster transaction processing. Networks like Ethereum, which transitioned to Ethereum 2.0 with PoS, benefit from improved scalability, reduced energy consumption, and a more secure and decentralized network, as validators are incentivized to act honestly, knowing they stand to lose their staked coins if they are found to be dishonest.

Delegated Proof of Stake (DPoS): Delegated Proof of Stake (DPoS) is an advanced variation of the traditional Proof of Stake (PoS) consensus mechanism, designed to improve transaction speed, scalability, and governance efficiency. In DPoS, coin holders do not directly validate transactions. Instead, they vote for delegates (or representatives), who are responsible for validating transactions, creating new blocks, and maintaining the overall integrity of the blockchain. The delegates are typically a smaller group of trusted participants, chosen through periodic elections, ensuring that the network is governed by a select few but still remains decentralized. By reducing the number of validators and concentrating the validation process in the hands of these elected delegates, DPoS significantly enhances transaction throughput and reduces the time it takes to confirm transactions, which can be a limitation in traditional PoS systems. This delegation system allows for faster block production and lower latency, making DPoS well-suited for platforms that require high scalability. Major blockchain platforms like EOS and TRON have adopted DPoS, as it enables them to process thousands of transactions per second while also providing a democratic governance model where the community has a say in who manages the network, enhancing the overall decentralization and security of the system.

The Role of Blockchain Nodes

Blockchain nodes are the backbone of the blockchain

network, enabling it to function in a decentralized manner. These nodes are responsible for maintaining and verifying the blockchain's data, making it possible for the blockchain to operate without a central authority.

Full Nodes, Light Nodes, and Miner Nodes

Full Nodes: A full node is a type of blockchain node that stores the entire blockchain and validates all transactions and blocks. Full nodes ensure that every transaction is legitimate and that the blockchain's rules are followed. Running a full node can be resource-intensive, as it requires storing a copy of the entire blockchain and continuously processing transactions.

Light Nodes: A light node (or "spv node," which stands for Simplified Payment Verification) does not store the full blockchain. Instead, it only stores the necessary information to verify transactions, such as the block headers. Light nodes are less resource-heavy and are often used by devices with limited storage or processing power, such as mobile phones or IoT devices.

Miner Nodes: Miner nodes are responsible for validating new transactions and adding them to the blockchain. Miners (in Proof of Work systems) compete to solve complex puzzles, and the first to succeed gets to add a new block to the chain and receive a reward. Miner nodes ensure the security of the blockchain by enforcing its consensus rules.

The Function of Blockchain Nodes in Maintaining Decentralization and Security

Blockchain nodes work together to maintain the integrity of the network. Each node is responsible for verifying the validity of transactions and blocks, ensuring that all copies of the blockchain are consistent. Since the blockchain is decentralized, no single entity controls the data, and nodes work together to reach consensus on the state of the blockchain. This structure ensures that the network is secure from attacks or manipulation. Importantly, the blockchain setup, including the rules for validation, consensus mechanisms, and participant roles, must be thoroughly defined and configured before the network begins operating. These rules set the foundation for how the blockchain will function and ensure that all participants adhere to the same standards, maintaining the integrity and security of the network from the start.

If one node or even a subset of nodes tries to alter the data, the rest of the network will reject the malicious changes due to the consensus mechanisms in place. By spreading the validation process across a wide array of nodes, blockchain networks become resistant to censorship, fraud, and single points of failure.

How Nodes Communicate and Share Data

Blockchain nodes communicate through a peer-to-peer (P2P) network, allowing direct interaction between nodes without a central authority. When a transaction is initiated, it is broadcast to the network and received by multiple nodes. Each node checks the transaction's validity by ensuring it adheres to the blockchain's rules, such as verifying the sender's funds and ensuring the transaction is properly signed. Once validated, the transaction is added to a block, which is then included in the blockchain by the appropriate nodes (e.g., miners or validators). This updated block becomes a permanent part of the ledger, ensuring that all participants have the same up-to-date version. This decentralized communication keeps the blockchain synchronized, meaning the network continues to function even if some nodes go offline.

Blockchain Beyond Cryptocurrency

While blockchain technology is most commonly associated with cryptocurrencies like Bitcoin and Ethereum, its potential stretches far beyond the financial world. Blockchain's decentralized and secure nature makes it ideal for a variety of applications, each of which could benefit from a system that removes intermediaries, enhances security, and promotes transparency.

Blockchain's Potential in Social Media, Content Distribution, and Decentralized Finance

Social Media: Blockchain can decentralize social media platforms, allowing users to own and control their own data. Platforms like Steemit use blockchain to reward users for creating and curating content, eliminating the need for centralized companies to control user data or monetize content. With blockchain-based social media, content creators and consumers can interact in a peer-to-peer manner, removing censorship and ensuring greater privacy.

Content Distribution: In the digital content industry, creators often face unfair revenue distribution due to intermediaries like streaming services or advertising platforms. Blockchain offers a way to bypass these intermediaries, enabling direct transactions between content creators and consumers. For instance, Audius is a blockchain-based music streaming service that allows artists to maintain full control over their music and earnings, providing a transparent, decentralized alternative to traditional music platforms.

Decentralized Finance (DeFi): DeFi is a rapidly growing sector in the blockchain space that aims to replace traditional financial services with decentralized alternatives. By leveraging blockchain and smart contracts, DeFi platforms allow users to borrow, lend, trade, and invest without relying on banks or financial institutions. These platforms, such as Uniswap (a decentralized exchange) and Compound (a decentralized lending platform), enable peer-to-peer financial services that are more accessible, efficient, and transparent.

Real-World Examples of Blockchain Use Cases Beyond Digital Currencies

Steemit: A blockchain-based social media platform where users are rewarded with cryptocurrency for posting and curating content. The system removes centralized control, giving content creators direct ownership and control over their work.

Audius: A decentralized music streaming platform that enables artists to directly distribute their music without relying on intermediaries. Audius utilizes blockchain to ensure transparency and fair revenue distribution.

DeFi Protocols: DeFi platforms like Aave, MakerDAO, and Compound are building decentralized alternatives to traditional financial services. These platforms enable lending, borrowing, and trading without intermediaries, lowering costs, increasing efficiency, and providing greater financial inclusion.

Blockchain's potential in fields like social media, content distribution, and finance represents just the tip of the iceberg. As more industries explore the advantages of decentralization, blockchain's impact will continue to grow and evolve, transforming the way we interact with digital information and services.

Chapter 2: Setting Up Your Linux Server

Why Linux for Blockchain Nodes?

When it comes to running blockchain nodes, Linux is often the operating system of choice for both individual users and organizations. Its stability, security, and open-source nature make it a perfect fit for blockchain technology. Here's why Linux stands out:

Advantages of Linux for Security, Reliability, and Cost-effectiveness

Security: Linux is well-known for its robust security features. It is inherently less vulnerable to attacks compared to other operating systems like Windows. Linux's permission model ensures that processes are isolated, preventing malware from easily compromising the entire system. Additionally, Linux offers advanced firewall and security tools, which are essential for protecting a blockchain node from external threats.

Reliability: Blockchain nodes require 24/7 uptime, and Linux's stability makes it ideal for this purpose. It can run continuously without experiencing performance degradation, and the operating system has a minimal risk of crashing. Linux servers are frequently used by large enterprises because of their reliability under heavy loads, which is essential when managing blockchain data.

Cost-effectiveness: As an open-source operating system, Linux is free to use. There are no licensing fees, which makes it more affordable than other proprietary systems like Windows. Additionally, the low resource overhead means that even older hardware can run blockchain nodes efficiently, reducing infrastructure costs.

Comparing Linux Distributions: Ubuntu, CentOS, and Debian

When setting up a Linux server for blockchain nodes, you have several distribution options.

While all Linux distributions offer similar core features, each has its strengths:

Debian: Debian is known for its stability and is a favorite among advanced Linux users and server administrators. It's the base distribution for Ubuntu, which makes it similar in many ways but less user-friendly. Debian's stability and minimalism make it an excellent choice for experienced users who want to control every aspect of their server setup, particularly for running blockchain nodes in production environments.

Ubuntu: Ubuntu is the most popular Linux distribution for both beginners and experienced users. It's known for its user-friendly interface, large community, and extensive support. Ubuntu also provides a wide range of pre-packaged software and is often the go-to choice for running blockchain nodes like Bitcoin and Ethereum. It's ideal for beginners because it has plenty of documentation and support forums.

CentOS: CentOS is a free and open-source version of Red Hat Enterprise Linux (RHEL). It is known for its stability and is commonly used in enterprise environments. CentOS is a great choice if you are running a blockchain node in a professional setting where stability and long-term support are essential. However, note that CentOS has shifted to CentOS Stream, which is a rolling release distribution, which may be less predictable than traditional CentOS.

Selecting Your Hardware

When running blockchain nodes, the hardware you use is a critical factor in ensuring performance and stability. The hardware requirements vary depending on whether you're running a mining node, full node, or light node.

Recommended Hardware Specifications for Different Use Cases

Mining Nodes

Mining requires high computational power, and the hardware specifications are more demanding.

For a mining setup:

CPU: High-performance multi-core processors (e.g., AMD Ryzen 9, Intel Core i9).

GPU: Graphics cards (GPUs) are crucial for mining cryptocurrencies that use Proof of Work, such as Ethereum. High-end GPUs (e.g., Nvidia RTX 3080, AMD Radeon RX 6800) are recommended.

RAM: At least 16 GB of RAM to ensure smooth operation.

Storage: A high-speed SSD with at least 500 GB of storage to handle mining software and the blockchain ledger.

Full Nodes

Running a full node means maintaining a complete copy of the blockchain and validating transactions.

This can be resource-intensive, especially with large blockchains like Bitcoin or Ethereum:

CPU: A mid-range multi-core processor (e.g., Intel Core i5 or i7, AMD Ryzen 5).

RAM: 8-16 GB of RAM to handle the operations efficiently.
Storage: You will need a large amount of disk space (500 GB to 2 TB or more) depending on the blockchain size. SSDs are highly recommended for faster data access and reduced latency.

Internet: A reliable and fast internet connection (at least 10 Mbps) is necessary for syncing and maintaining the blockchain.

Light Nodes
Light nodes store only part of the blockchain and rely on full nodes for transaction validation.

These are less resource-intensive:

CPU: Any modern CPU (e.g., Intel Core i3 or AMD Ryzen 3).

RAM: 4-8 GB of RAM.

Storage: At least 100 GB of storage for storing blockchain headers and partial data.

Internet: A stable internet connection with a speed of at least 5 Mbps.

Disk Space Considerations for Storing Blockchain Data

Blockchain data grows over time as more blocks are added to the chain. For full nodes, this can mean substantial disk space usage. For example, the Bitcoin blockchain has over 500 GB of data, and Ethereum's blockchain is even larger, requiring several terabytes of storage. If you're running a full node, you must plan for regular storage expansion.

Using SSDs is crucial for faster read/write speeds, which is essential for blockchain node operation. If your hardware supports it, using multiple drives in a RAID configuration can help improve redundancy and speed.

Ensuring Reliable Internet Connectivity

Blockchain nodes need a reliable and consistent internet connection for syncing and validating transactions. A slow or unstable connection can hinder the node's ability to validate transactions in a timely manner and contribute to network delays.

Ensure your internet connection has enough bandwidth to handle the demands of syncing and validating blocks. A fiber optic connection is ideal, but a stable DSL or cable connection with speeds of 10 Mbps or higher should be sufficient for most use cases.

Setting Up Your Linux Operating System

Once you've selected your hardware, the next step is to install and configure Linux to run your blockchain node. For a comprehensive guide on setting up a secure Linux server, you can refer to my book series, *The Linux Server Mastery Series*, available on Amazon.

Follow these steps for a smooth setup:

Installing Linux: Step-by-Step Guide to Installation

Choose a Linux Distribution: Select one of the Linux distributions discussed earlier, such as Debian, Ubuntu, or CentOS.

Download the ISO Image: Go to the official website of your chosen distribution and download the ISO file.

Create a Bootable USB Drive: Use tools like **Rufus** or **Etcher** to create a bootable USB drive with the downloaded ISO image.

Boot from USB: Insert the USB drive into the server, restart the machine, and boot from the USB.

Install Linux: Follow the on-screen instructions to install the operating system. Choose your preferred language, keyboard layout, and time zone.

Partition the Disk: Select the disk where you want to install Linux and partition it according to your needs (more on this in the next section).

Configure System Settings: Set up your root password, user accounts, and network configurations.

Reboot: After the installation is complete, remove the USB drive and reboot the system.

Configuring the System for Blockchain Tasks: Disk Partitioning, File Systems, and Encryption

Once the Linux operating system is installed to your satisfaction, configure the system for blockchain tasks:

Disk Partitioning for a Blockchain Node

After installing Linux, partitioning your disks is an important step in setting up a dedicated blockchain node. Partitioning helps you organize your disk space into separate sections for different uses, such as the operating system, blockchain data, and logs. This setup ensures that your blockchain data doesn't fill up your system partition, which could cause performance issues or even system instability.

Basic Steps for Partitioning Disks

Check the Available Disks:

Open a terminal and run the command lsblk or fdisk -l to list all the available disks and partitions. This will give you an overview of your current disk setup.

Choose the Disk to Partition:
Decide which disk you want to partition for your blockchain node. It is common to use a second disk (or a larger disk) for blockchain data, while the primary disk is reserved for the operating system.

Use fdisk or parted for Partitioning:
You can use fdisk (for MBR partitions) or parted (for GPT partitions) to create and manage partitions.

To begin partitioning, run sudo fdisk /dev/sdX, replacing /dev/sdX with the name of your target disk (e.g., /dev/sdb).

Create Partitions

Operating System Partition: This is typically the first partition where your Linux installation will reside. Choose a size that fits the OS and additional software.

Blockchain Data Partition: Allocate a large partition for blockchain data, as this will grow over time. The size depends on the blockchain you are running.

Log Partition: If you want to separate logs (such as blockchain node logs) from other data, create a smaller partition dedicated to logs. This prevents log files from filling up your main storage.

In fdisk, use the following commands to create partitions:

n to create a new partition.
p for primary partition.
Choose **partition type** (usually "**Linux**" or "**Linux filesystem**").
Assign partition sizes.
w to write the changes.

Format the Partitions:
After creating the partitions, format them using the appropriate file system (usually ext4 for Linux).

```
sudo mkfs.ext4 /dev/sdX1  # for the first partition
sudo mkfs.ext4 /dev/sdX2  # for the second partition
```

Replace /dev/sdX1 with the partition identifier you created earlier.

Mount the Partitions:
Once the partitions are formatted, mount them to appropriate directories (e.g., /mnt/blkdata for blockchain data and /mnt/logs for logs).

```
sudo mkdir /mnt/blkdata
sudo mount /dev/sdX2 /mnt/blkdata
sudo mkdir /mnt/logs
sudo mount /dev/sdX3 /mnt/logs
```

Update /etc/fstab:
To ensure the partitions are mounted automatically on

system reboot, add them to /etc/fstab.

sudo nano /etc/fstab

Add entries like:

/dev/sdX2 /mnt/blkdata ext4 defaults 0 2
/dev/sdX3 /mnt/logs ext4 defaults 0 2

Save and exit the editor.

Verify the Setup:
Run df -h to check that the partitions are mounted correctly and that they are using the expected disk space.

By partitioning the disk in this way, you create a cleaner, more organized system where each component of your blockchain node (OS, data, and logs) is kept separate. This can help prevent issues where the blockchain's growing data might impact the stability or performance of the system, and allows for easier management of disk space over time.

File Systems: Ext4 is the most commonly used file system for Linux, but you can also use XFS or Btrfs depending on your needs. If you're working with large amounts of data, XFS or Btrfs might be more suitable for managing large files and directories efficiently.

Encryption: Encrypt your disk partitions to protect sensitive blockchain data. Tools like LUKS (Linux Unified Key Setup) can be used to encrypt partitions at the hardware level, adding an extra layer of security.

Securing Your Server

Securing your blockchain server is critical to prevent unauthorized access and protect your node's data.

Hardening the Server: Basic Security Measures (SSH, Firewalls, and Updating Software)

SSH: Configure SSH (Secure Shell) to access the server remotely. Disable root login via SSH to ensure that only authorized users can log in. Use public-key authentication for added security, rather than relying on password authentication.

Firewalls: Set up a firewall (e.g., UFW, Iptables, or NFTables) to restrict incoming and outgoing traffic. Only allow necessary ports, such as the ones used by your blockchain node. Close all other ports to reduce the attack surface.

Software Updates: Regularly update the operating system and software packages to ensure you have the latest security patches. Use tools like apt (Ubuntu/Debian) or yum (CentOS) to automate the process.

Using VPNs and Encryption for Additional Privacy

For added security and privacy, consider using a VPN (Virtual Private Network) to encrypt your internet connection and mask your IP address when interacting with the blockchain network. VPNs are especially important if you're running a public node and want to ensure your location and identity are kept private.

Encryption tools like OpenVPN or WireGuard can help set up a secure tunnel for your blockchain node to communicate safely with other nodes in the network.

Chapter 3: Installing and Running Blockchain Nodes

Choosing the Right Blockchain Software

When running a blockchain node, one of the first decisions you'll face is choosing the appropriate blockchain software to install. The software you choose will determine the blockchain network your node will connect to and what kind of functionality your node will provide.

Overview of Popular Blockchain Networks

Bitcoin: The first and most well-known cryptocurrency, Bitcoin operates on a decentralized peer-to-peer network. The Bitcoin network uses a Proof of Work (PoW) consensus algorithm to verify transactions and secure the network. Running a Bitcoin node ensures that you're contributing to the security and decentralization of the Bitcoin network, and you'll have access to the entire Bitcoin blockchain history.

Ethereum: Ethereum is a decentralized platform that allows developers to create and deploy smart contracts and decentralized applications (dApps). Ethereum uses a Proof of Stake (PoS) consensus mechanism (following the Ethereum 2.0 upgrade). Running an Ethereum node connects you to one of the largest and most versatile blockchain ecosystems in the world, with capabilities far beyond just cryptocurrency transactions.

Litecoin: Often considered the silver to Bitcoin's gold, Litecoin is a faster and more efficient cryptocurrency. It uses a similar Proof of Work (PoW) consensus mechanism but with a shorter block generation time and different hashing algorithm (Scrypt). Litecoin nodes contribute to the network's security while offering faster transactions than Bitcoin.

Ripple (XRP): Ripple focuses on facilitating real-time, cross-border payments for financial institutions. It uses a unique consensus algorithm called the RippleNet Protocol, which relies on trusted validators to confirm transactions. Ripple is designed for scalability, with much faster transaction speeds and lower fees compared to Bitcoin and Ethereum, making it a popular choice for global payment networks.

Cardano: Cardano is a blockchain platform designed for the development of secure and scalable dApps, similar to Ethereum, but with a focus on peer-reviewed research and formal verification. Cardano uses a Proof of Stake (PoS) consensus algorithm called Ouroboros, which is designed to be highly secure and energy-efficient. Running a Cardano node connects you to a network that prioritizes sustainability and scientific rigor in its approach.

Polkadot: Polkadot is a multi-chain blockchain platform that allows various blockchains to interoperate and share information. It uses a nominated Proof of Stake (nPoS) consensus mechanism to achieve consensus across its relay chain and connected parachains. Polkadot is designed to support the development of decentralized applications with a focus on scalability and cross-chain communication.

Solana: Solana is a high-performance blockchain designed to support decentralized applications (dApps) and crypto-currencies at scale. It uses a combination of Proof of History (PoH) and Proof of Stake (PoS) to achieve lightning-fast transaction speeds and low costs. Solana has gained popularity for its ability to handle a high throughput of transactions, making it ideal for decentralized finance (DeFi) and other high-demand applications.

Other Blockchains: There are many other emerging blockchains, each with unique features, goals, and use cases. For example, Tezos focuses on self-amending smart contracts, Avalanche prioritizes scalability and high-speed transaction finality, and Binance Smart Chain is optimized for low-cost, high-speed dApps. Understanding the specific use case of each blockchain will help you decide which one aligns with your interests and goals.

Deciding Which Blockchain Software to Run on Your Server

Once you've decided which blockchain you'd like to connect to, you'll need to choose the corresponding software to run on your server.

Here are some examples of the most widely-used software for popular blockchains:

Bitcoin Core: The reference implementation for the Bitcoin network. Bitcoin Core is a full node software that downloads the entire blockchain and validates transactions. It provides a high level of security and privacy but requires significant disk space and bandwidth to run.

Geth (Go-Ethereum): Geth is the official Go implementation of the Ethereum protocol. It can be used to run an Ethereum full node, interact with smart contracts, or even mine Ethereum (though mining is transitioning away from Proof of Work to Proof of Stake). Geth provides both a command-line interface and an RPC API for interacting with the network.

Litecoin Core: Similar to Bitcoin Core, Litecoin Core is the official full node software for the Litecoin network. It allows users to participate in the Litecoin network, verify transactions, and maintain a copy of the entire blockchain.

Other Blockchain Clients: Depending on the blockchain you choose to run, there may be other clients or software options available, such as Parity for Ethereum or Bitcoin Cash Node for Bitcoin Cash. It's important to choose a well-supported client with active development and a large community for troubleshooting.

Installing Blockchain Software on Linux

Now that you've chosen the blockchain software that best fits your needs, it's time to install it on your Linux server. Below are the installation steps for Bitcoin Core and Geth, two of the most popular blockchain clients.

Step-by-Step Installation for Different Blockchain Software

Bitcoin Core Installation (on Ubuntu/Debian):

Update Your System: Make sure your system is up-to-date with the latest security patches.

```
sudo apt update
sudo apt upgrade
```

Install Dependencies - Bitcoin Core requires several dependencies. Install them using the following command:

```
sudo apt install build-essential libtool autotools-dev automake pkg-config libssl-dev libevent-dev bsdmainutils libboost-all-dev libzmq3-dev libdb-dev libminiupnpc-dev libprotobuf-dev protobuf-compiler libqt5core5a libqt5gui5 libqt5widgets5 qt5-qmake qtbase5-dev qtchooser libhidapi-dev libgmp-dev
```

These dependencies are listed below in a more readable format, for clarity:

build-essential
libtool
autotools-dev
automake
pkg-config
libssl-dev
libevent-dev
bsdmainutils
libboost-all-dev
libzmq3-dev
libdb-dev
libminiupnpc-dev
libprotobuf-dev
protobuf-compiler
libqt5core5a
libqt5gui5
libqt5widgets5
qt5-qmake
qtbase5-dev
qtchooser
libhidapi-dev
libgmp-dev

Download Bitcoin Core: Visit the official Bitcoin website (https://bitcoin.org/en/download) and download the latest stable release.

wget **https://bitcoincore.org/bin/bitcoin-core-22.0/bitcoin-22.0-x86_64-linux-gnu.tar.gz**

tar -xzvf **bitcoin-22.0-x86_64-linux-gnu.tar.gz**

Run Bitcoin Core: Navigate to the directory where Bitcoin Core is extracted and run the Bitcoin daemon.

```
cd bitcoin-22.0/bin
./bitcoind
```

Initial Setup: Bitcoin Core will begin downloading the blockchain, which may take some time depending on your internet connection and hardware. The blockchain data is stored in the ~/.bitcoin directory by default.

Geth (Go-Ethereum) Installation (on Ubuntu/Debian):

Install Geth via PPA:

```
sudo add-apt-repository -y ppa:ethereum/ethereum
sudo apt update
sudo apt install geth
```

Start Geth: Once installed, you can start Geth and synchronize it with the Ethereum network.

```
geth --syncmode "fast" --datadir /path/to/ethereum/data
```

Geth will begin downloading the Ethereum blockchain and syncing with the network.

Interact with the Ethereum Network: You can interact with Geth via the console or by using the JSON-RPC interface. For example, to open the Geth JavaScript console:

```
geth console
```

Configuring the Node to Connect to the Blockchain Network

After installation, you'll need to configure the node to connect to the respective blockchain network.

Here are some configuration tips:

Bitcoin Core: Bitcoin Core can be configured using a configuration file called bitcoin.conf. The file is located in the ~/.bitcoin directory. You can modify settings such as the RPC user, port, and other options here.

Example configuration:

```
rpcuser=yourusername
rpcpassword=yourpassword
server=1
daemon=1
```

Geth: Geth has various options to configure the node's behavior. You can use command-line flags to set up the node's syncing mode, data directory, and network (mainnet or testnet).

Example:

```
geth --syncmode "fast" --networkid 1 --datadir /path/to/data
```

Once configured, your node will begin syncing with the respective network. Keep in mind that the initial sync can take days or even weeks, depending on the blockchain size and your internet connection speed.

Understanding Blockchain Syncing

When you run a blockchain node, syncing is the process by which your node downloads and verifies the entire blockchain or a portion of it, depending on whether it is a full node or light node. Understanding how syncing works is crucial to ensure your node is functioning correctly.

How Nodes Sync with the Blockchain Network

Nodes sync with the blockchain network by connecting to other peers in the network. These peers help the node download and verify blocks, transactions, and other data.

There are different methods of syncing:

Full Sync: A full node downloads and verifies every block from the genesis block (the first block) onward. This process ensures that the node has the complete history of the blockchain and can independently verify all transactions.

Fast Sync: In fast sync mode (used by Geth), the node skips the verification of older blocks and only downloads the most recent state of the blockchain. This allows the node to sync faster, but it doesn't have the entire blockchain history.

Light Sync: A light node only downloads the headers of blocks and relies on full nodes to fetch transaction data. Light nodes are much faster to sync, but they don't validate transactions themselves and must trust full nodes for accurate information.

Resolving Common Syncing Issues and Troubleshooting Techniques

Slow Syncing: If syncing is unusually slow, check your internet connection and make sure it's stable and fast enough. Additionally, consider switching to a faster syncing mode (e.g., fast sync in Geth). You may also want to ensure you're connecting to healthy peers.

Out of Sync Errors: Sometimes, your node may show a "syncing error" or be stuck at a particular block. This could be due to misconfigured settings or an issue with the peer-to-peer network. Restarting the node or checking for the latest software updates may resolve these issues.

Low Disk Space: Running a full node requires substantial disk space, and you may run into issues if your server's storage is running low. Ensure that your disk has enough space for the blockchain data. If necessary, you can increase the disk size or switch to a larger hard drive.

Firewall or Network Issues: If your node cannot connect to other peers, check your firewall settings to ensure the necessary ports (typically 8333 for Bitcoin and 30303 for Ethereum) are open. You may need to adjust your server's firewall or router settings to allow for inbound and outbound traffic.

Chapter 4: Securing Your Blockchain Node

Hardening Your Linux Server for Blockchain Use

Security is paramount when running a blockchain node, as your server will interact with the global blockchain network, storing and transmitting sensitive data. Ensuring the safety of your Linux server requires implementing a series of advanced security measures to protect it from potential threats.

Advanced Security Measures: Firewalls, Intrusion Detection, and Monitoring

Firewalls: A firewall serves as a security barrier between your server and external networks, regulating the incoming and outgoing traffic based on predefined rules. It helps protect your server from unauthorized access and potential attacks by ensuring only trusted traffic is allowed. On Linux, you can configure firewalls using tools like UFW (Uncomplicated Firewall), which simplifies rule management, or more advanced tools like IPtables and NFTables, which offer greater control and flexibility for more complex network configurations. Properly configuring a firewall is a crucial first step in securing your blockchain node and preventing malicious traffic from reaching your server.

Example using UFW:

```
sudo ufw allow 8333/tcp  # Bitcoin default port
sudo ufw allow 30303/tcp  # Ethereum default port
sudo ufw enable
sudo ufw status
```

In this example, UFW (Uncomplicated Firewall) is being used to allow incoming traffic on the default ports for Bitcoin (8333/tcp) and Ethereum (30303/tcp). After allowing the ports, the firewall is enabled, and the status can be checked using ufw status.

Example using IPtables:

```
# Bitcoin default port
sudo iptables -A INPUT -p tcp --dport 8333 -j ACCEPT

# Ethereum default port
sudo iptables -A INPUT -p tcp --dport 30303 -j ACCEPT

# Save the rules to persist on reboot
sudo iptables-save > /etc/iptables/rules.v4

# Check the current firewall rules
sudo iptables -L
```

This example shows how to use IPtables to allow incoming traffic on Bitcoin and Ethereum ports. The -A INPUT command adds rules to the input chain, and -j ACCEPT allows traffic for those specific ports. The rules are saved to ensure they persist across reboots.

Example using NFTables:

```
# Bitcoin default port
sudo nft add rule inet filter input tcp dport 8333 accept

# Ethereum default port
sudo nft add rule inet filter input tcp dport 30303 accept

# List the current ruleset
sudo nft list ruleset
```

Here, NFTables is used to add rules for Bitcoin and Ethereum ports. nft add rule inet filter input defines a rule for the input chain of the inet family, and tcp dport specifies the port to accept. nft list ruleset displays the current rules.

Important: Open only the necessary ports for the blockchain software you are running (e.g., Bitcoin's default port is 8333). Keep in mind that opening unnecessary ports can expose your server to attacks.

Intrusion Detection Systems (IDS): An IDS helps detect suspicious activity on your server, such as unusual login attempts, excessive data transfers, or unauthorized access. Tools like Snort and OSSEC can be installed on Linux to monitor and log potentially malicious activities.

Example of installing Snort:

sudo apt-get install snort

IDS tools help ensure that any attempts to compromise your node are detected in real-time, allowing you to take swift action.

Monitoring: Regular monitoring of your server is essential for identifying vulnerabilities and performance issues. Tools like Nagios, Zabbix, and Prometheus can help monitor the health of your node by tracking metrics such as uptime, disk usage, and CPU load.

Example with Nagios:
sudo apt-get install nagios3

Set up alerts to notify you if any performance or security issues arise, ensuring timely intervention.

Setting Up Secure Access to Your Node (SSH Key Management)

SSH Keys: For secure, encrypted access to your server, use SSH (Secure Shell) with key-based authentication instead of password-based logins. SSH key pairs consist of a private key (stored securely on your local machine) and a public key (stored on the server).

To generate an SSH key pair:

```
ssh-keygen -t rsa -b 4096
```

After generating the key pair, copy the public key to your server:

```
ssh-copy-id user@your-server-ip
```

This method eliminates the risk of brute-force password attacks and enhances the overall security of your node.

Disable Password Authentication: After configuring SSH key authentication, it's a good idea to disable password-based logins for extra security.

Edit the SSH configuration file:

```
sudo nano /etc/ssh/sshd_config
```

Change the line:

```
#PasswordAuthentication yes
```

Change it to:

```
PasswordAuthentication no
```

Restart the SSH service:

```
sudo systemctl restart sshd
```

Restricting SSH Access by IP: For even tighter security, limit SSH access to specific IP addresses or IP ranges by configuring the firewall or SSH settings.

Managing System Updates and Ensuring the Server is Patched

Regular updates are essential to secure your server. Linux distributions frequently release security patches to address vulnerabilities, and it's important to apply these updates promptly.

Automated Updates: To keep your system up to date, enable automatic security updates on your Linux server:

```
sudo apt-get install unattended-upgrades
sudo dpkg-reconfigure --priority=low unattended-upgrades
```

This will automatically install security patches for critical packages, minimizing the window of exposure to security risks.

Manual Updates - You can manually update the system by running the following commands:

```
sudo apt update
sudo apt upgrade
```

Regularly check for updates to your blockchain software (e.g., Bitcoin Core, Geth) and apply them as soon as they are available.

Securing Blockchain Data

Your blockchain node stores critical data, such as private keys, wallet information, and transaction histories. Protecting this data from unauthorized access is essential.

How to Securely Store Private Keys and Wallets

Private Key Security: The private key is the most sensitive piece of information in the blockchain world. It allows you to access and control your assets, and anyone with access to it can potentially steal them. Therefore, it's crucial to keep private keys offline and away from the server when not in use.

Cold Storage: Use cold storage methods (offline wallets) for storing private keys. Hardware wallets like Ledger and Trezor are widely used to securely store private keys away from the server.

Avoid Storing Private Keys on the Server: If you must store private keys on the server (which is not recommended), make sure the server is encrypted and the keys are stored in secure, encrypted locations (e.g., using a KeePass vault or similar).

Wallet Protection: Always use strong passwords to encrypt wallets, and back up wallet files to a secure external location (such as an encrypted USB drive or cloud storage with strong encryption).

Best Practices for Encrypting Sensitive Data

Full Disk Encryption: Implement full disk encryption (FDE) using tools like LUKS or dm-crypt to ensure that even if your server is compromised, the data on it remains inaccessible without the correct decryption key.

Example to encrypt a disk using LUKS:

```
sudo cryptsetup luksFormat /dev/sda1
sudo cryptsetup luksOpen /dev/sda1 myencrypteddisk
```

Ensure the disk is mounted and encrypted at boot time by configuring **/etc/crypttab** and **/etc/fstab**.

Encrypt Wallet Files: Use encryption tools like GPG to encrypt sensitive wallet files or private keys. This ensures that even if someone gains unauthorized access to the server, they cannot access your critical data without the decryption key.

Example to encrypt a wallet with GPG:

```
gpg --output wallet.gpg --encrypt --recipient your-email
wallet.dat
```

Using Hardware Wallets for Extra Protection

Hardware wallets are considered one of the most secure ways to store cryptocurrency, as they are physical devices that are never connected to the internet, minimizing exposure to online threats. These wallets support a variety of blockchain networks and are highly resistant to malware and hacking attempts.

Popular Hardware Wallets: The most common hardware wallets are Ledger Nano S/X, Trezor, and KeepKey. These wallets store private keys securely and require physical confirmation to perform any transaction, adding an additional layer of protection.

Integrating Hardware Wallets: When using a hardware wallet with your blockchain node, you can interact with it via the wallet's interface, ensuring that private keys never leave the hardware device.

Monitoring Your Blockchain Node

Once your node is running and secured, it's essential to regularly monitor its health and performance to ensure it operates smoothly and remains secure. Continuous monitoring helps verify that your node is fully synchronized with the blockchain network, meaning it has the latest data and is correctly processing transactions. It also allows you to track resource usage, such as CPU, memory, and disk space, to ensure the node is not overburdened, which could lead to slow performance or crashes. Additionally, monitoring can help detect potential security threats, such as unusual login attempts or abnormal network traffic, allowing you to respond quickly to any malicious activity. Regular checks and updates help maintain the efficiency and integrity of your node, ensuring it contributes effectively to the blockchain network while safeguarding against disruptions or vulnerabilities.

Setting Up Monitoring Tools for Node Health

Uptime and Sync Status: Use tools like Prometheus and Grafana to monitor uptime, sync status, and the health of your blockchain node. These tools can be configured to display metrics such as block height, peer connections, and CPU usage.

Example Prometheus setup:

```
sudo apt-get install prometheus
```

Prometheus can scrape metrics from your node (if supported) or from custom endpoints that track the node's sync and status.

Alerting and Notifications: Set up alerting systems using Zabbix or Nagios to send notifications when your node goes offline, falls out of sync, or experiences performance degradation.

Using Log Management Tools to Track Blockchain Node Activity

Syslog: Linux servers use syslog to store log messages. Use this system to track and analyze blockchain node activity, such as transactions, peers, or errors. Regular log review helps identify potential issues early.

To review logs:

```
sudo tail -f /var/log/syslog
```

Journal: Debian-based systems, including Debian itself, use systemd's journal for logging instead of the traditional syslog. This system logs messages generated by the operating system, services, and applications, including blockchain node activity such as transactions, peer connections, or errors. Regular log review using journalctl can help you monitor your node's health, identify issues, and troubleshoot problems more efficiently.

To review logs with journalctl:

sudo journalctl -f

This command will display real-time logs, allowing you to track any activity or errors on your blockchain node. You can also filter logs by specific services or dates to focus on particular information relevant to your node's operation.

Log Analysis Tools: Implement centralized logging solutions such as ELK Stack (Elasticsearch, Logstash, and Kibana) to aggregate, analyze, and visualize logs from your blockchain node. This makes it easier to identify patterns or abnormal activities.

Example ELK installation:

sudo apt-get install elasticsearch logstash kibana

By continuously monitoring and analyzing log data, you can identify potential vulnerabilities or irregular behaviors in your blockchain node, ensuring a high level of security and efficiency.

Chapter 5: Running a Cryptocurrency Node

Bitcoin and Ethereum Nodes

Running a Bitcoin or Ethereum node allows you to participate directly in the blockchain network. These nodes support the decentralized infrastructure by verifying transactions, relaying information, and maintaining a full copy of the blockchain. In this section, we'll cover how to install and configure Bitcoin and Ethereum nodes on Linux.

Installing Bitcoin Core and Geth (Ethereum) on Linux

Bitcoin Core Installation

Bitcoin Core is the reference implementation of the Bitcoin protocol and serves as a full node.

To install Bitcoin Core on a Linux system:

Update your package list:

sudo apt-get update

Install Bitcoin Core dependencies:

sudo apt-get install build-essential libtool autotools-dev pkg-config libssl-dev libevent-dev bsdmainutils libboost-all-dev

For a more readable list of these dependencies:
build-essencial
libtool
autotools-dev
pkg-config
libssl-dev
libevent-dev
bsdmainutils
libboost-all-dev

Download and install Bitcoin Core:

wget **https://bitcoincore.org/bin/bitcoin-core-22.0/bitcoin-22.0-x86_64-linux-gnu.tar.gz**

tar -xvf **bitcoin-22.0-x86_64-linux-gnu.tar.gz**

cd bitcoin-22.0

sudo install -m 0755 -o root -g root -t /usr/local/bin bin/*

Start Bitcoin Core:

bitcoind -daemon

Bitcoin Core is now running as a full node, verifying transactions and blocks.

Geth (Ethereum) Installation: Geth is the Go-based client for Ethereum, allowing you to run a full Ethereum node. To install Geth on Linux:

Update your package list:

sudo apt-get update

Install the Geth dependencies:

sudo apt-get install software-properties-common
sudo add-apt-repository -y ppa:ethereum/ethereum
sudo apt-get update
sudo apt-get install Ethereum

Start Geth and sync with the Ethereum network:

geth --syncmode "fast" --cache=1024

Your Ethereum node will begin syncing with the network, downloading the latest block data.

Configuring Your Node as a Full Node, Miner, or Validator

Full Node: Both Bitcoin Core and Geth are configured as full nodes by default. Full nodes maintain a complete copy of the blockchain, validate transactions, and ensure the network's security by independently verifying transactions and blocks.

They check for validity by verifying signatures, preventing double-spending, and ensuring blocks are properly linked. Full nodes help maintain decentralization by rejecting invalid transactions and blocks, supporting the integrity of the blockchain. They also store the entire blockchain history, allowing users to verify past transactions and network status.

Running a full node requires syncing with the blockchain, which can take time and space. Once synced, it operates autonomously, ensuring security and contributing to network decentralization. Full nodes are more secure and private than light nodes because they do not rely on third-party verification.

Mining Node (for Bitcoin): To turn your Bitcoin node into a miner, install mining software like CGMiner or BFGMiner and configure it with your node. Mining contributes to the Bitcoin network by verifying and adding transactions to the blockchain, earning miners rewards in newly minted bitcoins and transaction fees.

Mining is vital for maintaining the network's decentralization and security through the Proof of Work (PoW) consensus algorithm. Miners solve cryptographic puzzles to validate transactions, ensuring the integrity of the blockchain.

Some mine for financial gain, while others do it to support Bitcoin's decentralized principles. However, mining requires substantial computational power and electricity, so it's important to evaluate its cost-effectiveness and environmental impact.

To start mining with your node, install mining software like CGMiner or BFGMiner, configure it properly, and join a mining pool (if you prefer collective mining) to increase your chances of earning rewards.

For example:

Install CGMiner:

sudo apt-get install cgminer

Configure CGMiner with your node's details and a mining pool:

cgminer -o stratum+tcp://pool.address:port -u yourUsername -p yourPassword

Validator Node (for Ethereum): For Ethereum, you can configure your node as a validator if you want to participate in Proof of Stake (PoS). To do this, you'll need to run a staking client like Prysm or Lighthouse.

Example with Prysm:

Install the Prysm validator client:
curl -Lo prysm.sh
https://github.com/prysmaticlabs/prysm/releases/download/v2.0.0-
alpha.16/prysm-2.0.0-alpha.16-linux-amd64

chmod +x prysm.sh

Start the validator:
./prysm.sh validator

How to Interact with the Blockchain: Sending and Receiving Transactions

Bitcoin

Sending Bitcoin: Use the Bitcoin Core command line or wallet interface to send Bitcoin.

bitcoin-cli sendtoaddress "recipient_address" amount

Receiving Bitcoin: Generate a new address using:

bitcoin-cli getnewaddress

Share this address with the person sending you Bitcoin.

Ethereum

Sending Ethereum: You can send Ethereum from your node using Geth's eth_sendTransaction method.

```
geth attach
personal.sendTransaction({from: 'your_address', to:
'recipient_address', value: web3.toWei(1, 'ether')})
```

Receiving Ethereum - Generate an address in your Ethereum account with:

```
geth account new
```

Setting Up a Mining Node (Optional)

Running a mining node enables you to contribute to the creation of new blocks on the blockchain by solving complex computational puzzles in the Proof of Work (PoW) consensus algorithm. In this section, we'll explore how to set up mining hardware and software to connect to your node.

What is Mining? The Role of Miners in the Blockchain Network

Mining is the process by which new transactions are verified and added to the blockchain. In the Proof of Work system (used by Bitcoin), miners compete to solve a cryptographic puzzle, and the first one to solve it gets to add a new block to the blockchain and is rewarded with cryptocurrency.

Bitcoin: Bitcoin mining involves using computational power to solve SHA-256 cryptographic puzzles. The first miner to solve the puzzle gets rewarded with Bitcoin.

Ethereum: Ethereum mining uses the Ethash algorithm to verify transactions and create new blocks.

How to Set Up Mining Hardware and Connect It to Your Node

Mining Hardware: Mining requires significant computational resources. Most miners use specialized hardware called ASICs (Application-Specific Integrated Circuits) for Bitcoin, as they are highly efficient at solving cryptographic puzzles. For Ethereum, miners typically use GPUs (Graphics Processing Units) because they can perform the necessary computations more efficiently.

Setting Up ASICs: If you're mining Bitcoin, connect your ASIC miners to the internet and configure them to connect to your mining pool.

Example:

Connect the miner to your router via Ethernet.

Access the miner's web interface through your browser (using the IP address provided by the miner).

Enter your mining pool details and start mining.

Setting Up GPUs for Ethereum Mining: Install mining software like Claymore or PhoenixMiner to use your GPU for Ethereum mining.

After setting up the mining software:

Configure the software to connect to your mining pool.

Start mining using:

./ethminer -G -S eth.pool.address:port -O yourEthereumWalletAddress

Mining Software and Configuring the Node for Mining

Bitcoin Mining Software: Use mining software **like CGMiner or BFGMiner** to connect to your Bitcoin node and mining pool. Configure the software with your node's details and the mining pool's information.

Ethereum Mining Software: Ethereum miners can use Ethminer or Claymore to connect to the Ethereum blockchain. These software tools interact with your Ethereum node and mining pool to contribute hashing power to the network.

Understanding Cryptocurrency Rewards

Whether you're mining or staking, nodes can earn cryptocurrency rewards for their efforts in securing the network. Mining involves using computational power to solve complex mathematical puzzles, validating transactions, and adding them to the blockchain. Miners are rewarded with newly minted coins and transaction fees. Staking, on the other hand, involves locking up a certain amount of cryptocurrency in a wallet to support the operations of a blockchain network. Stakers help validate transactions and secure the network in exchange for rewards, often in the form of additional coins or tokens. Both methods contribute to the security, decentralization, and integrity of blockchain networks.

How Nodes are Rewarded in Proof of Work and Proof of Stake Systems

Proof of Work (PoW): In PoW systems like Bitcoin, miners are rewarded with newly minted coins (block rewards) and transaction fees for successfully mining a new block. The reward decreases over time, such as Bitcoin's halving event that occurs roughly every four years, reducing the reward by half.

Bitcoin Reward: As of now, the reward for mining a block on the Bitcoin network is 6.25 BTC, but this will decrease with each halving event.

Proof of Stake (PoS): In PoS systems like Ethereum (post-Merge), validators are rewarded for proposing and validating blocks. Instead of computational power, PoS relies on the amount of cryptocurrency a user has "staked" as collateral.

Ethereum Reward: Stakers (validators) receive transaction fees and a portion of the newly minted ETH for validating blocks.

How to Monitor Earnings from Mining or Staking

Mining Earnings: To monitor your mining rewards, you can use mining pool dashboards or tools like NiceHash or F2Pool, which display metrics such as hash rate, shares submitted, and rewards earned.

Staking Earnings: For Ethereum staking, you can use tools like Eth2.0 Beacon Chain explorer or Prysm's Web UI to monitor your validator rewards, check your staking performance, and ensure that your node is participating correctly in block validation.

Example:

```
geth attach
eth.getBlock('latest').reward
```

By setting up and running a cryptocurrency node, you are not only helping to secure and decentralize the network but also have the potential to earn rewards through mining or staking. The rewards vary depending on the network's consensus mechanism (PoW or PoS), but the process of contributing to the network remains the same.

Chapter 6: Using Blockchain for Social Media

Decentralized Social Media

Social media has revolutionized the way people connect, share, and communicate. However, as these platforms have grown, centralized social media networks have faced numerous challenges. Blockchain technology presents a decentralized solution that can address these issues and bring new opportunities for social interaction.

The Limitations of Centralized Social Media Platforms

Large centralized social media platforms, such as Facebook, Twitter, and Instagram, have numerous limitations that affect both users and creators:

Data Privacy Issues: These platforms control vast amounts of personal data, which has led to privacy concerns. Data breaches, surveillance, and misuse of personal information are major issues on centralized platforms.

Censorship: Centralized platforms are subject to censorship by governments and corporations, often leading to the removal of content or banning users without clear justification. This can stifle free expression and limit the diversity of voices online.

Monetization and Control: Centralized social media platforms benefit financially by collecting user data and serving targeted advertisements. Content creators often struggle to monetize their work, with platforms taking a large share of the revenue.

Lack of Transparency: Decisions regarding content removal, shadow banning, and algorithm changes are often opaque. Users have little control over their presence and content on these platforms.

Blockchain-based social media platforms seek to address these issues by providing decentralized, transparent, and user-controlled alternatives.

Blockchain-Based Social Media Platforms (e.g., Steemit, Hive, etc.)

Blockchain technology offers several advantages for social media platforms:

Decentralization: Blockchain-based social platforms are decentralized, meaning there is no central authority controlling user data or content. This ensures that users maintain control over their own data and can communicate without interference from a central entity.

Immutability: Content published on a blockchain is permanent and cannot be altered or deleted. This is particularly important for ensuring the free expression of ideas and protecting content from censorship.

Incentivization: Many blockchain-based social platforms use cryptocurrency to reward users for their contributions. For example, users can earn tokens for posting, commenting, or upvoting content. This creates a more equitable distribution of value within the platform.

Examples of Blockchain-Based Social Platforms:

Steemit: A decentralized blogging and social networking platform that uses the Steem blockchain. Users can earn cryptocurrency by publishing posts, commenting, and voting on content.

Hive: A hard fork of Steemit that continues the vision of decentralized social media. Hive focuses on community governance and offers similar features to Steemit, with an emphasis on speed and scalability.

Running Your Own Social Media Node: Benefits and Setup

Running your own node on a decentralized social media platform like Steemit or Hive gives you greater control over the platform's operations and allows you to participate directly in the blockchain ecosystem. By running a node, you become part of the network that validates transactions and stores data, contributing to the security and decentralization of the platform.

Benefits:

Earn Rewards: Running your own node can provide rewards in the form of cryptocurrency, as nodes may receive a portion of the network's tokens for validating posts, comments, and interactions.

Governance Participation: Many decentralized platforms allow node operators to participate in governance, voting on decisions about the platform's future direction.

Increased Control: Running a node gives you more control over your data, privacy, and interactions on the platform.

Setup: Setting up your own node for decentralized social media typically involves the following steps:

Choose a Platform: Decide whether you want to run a node for Steemit, Hive, or another decentralized platform.

Install Node Software: Download and install the node software for the chosen platform. For example, for Hive, you can use hived (Hive's full node software).

Synchronize the Blockchain: Once the node software is installed, it needs to sync with the blockchain. This process can take some time depending on the blockchain's size.

Maintain the Node: Keep your node updated with the latest software and monitor its health to ensure it's running smoothly.

Setting Up a Steemit or Hive Node

Setting up a node for decentralized social platforms like Steemit or Hive allows you to participate in content creation, validation, and the overall governance of the platform. Here's a step-by-step guide to setting up your own node.

Step-by-Step Guide to Setting Up a Node for Decentralized Social Platforms

Install Dependencies: Start by installing the required dependencies. For Hive, you'll need to install software such as hived and ensure that your server is running the necessary environment (e.g., Ubuntu 20.04, Docker, etc.).

sudo apt-get update

```
sudo apt-get install build-essential cmake git libboost-all-dev
libssl-dev
```

Clone the Node Repository: Clone the repository for the blockchain software. For Hive, this can be done by cloning the Hive repository from GitHub:

```
git clone https://github.com/steemit/hive.git
cd hive
```

Build the Node: Compile the node software from the source code.

```
cmake .
make
```

Start the Node: Once the node software is built, you can start the node. For Hive:

```
./hived --rpc-endpoint=localhost:8090
```

Sync the Node: The node will need to sync with the blockchain. This process may take several hours or days, depending on the size of the blockchain and your server's performance.

Configuring and Managing Posts, Comments, and Upvotes on the Blockchain

Once the node is successfully set up and synchronized with the blockchain, it will begin its crucial role in validating and managing various types of content, including posts, comments, and upvotes. These actions are typically represented as transactions within the blockchain, ensuring that every post, comment, and upvote is securely recorded, immutable, and can be traced back to its origin.

To configure the node for this task, you'll need to ensure that it is properly connected to the relevant smart contract or decentralized application (dApp) responsible for handling social interactions on the blockchain. The node will check the validity of new posts, ensuring they adhere to the platform's rules and that they are associated with an active user account. It will also validate comments, ensuring they are linked to the appropriate posts and conform to community guidelines.

Upvotes, which serve as a form of social validation, will also be processed by the node. The system will verify that the upvotes are legitimate (i.e., not coming from fake or duplicate accounts) and that they are properly recorded on the blockchain.

Additionally, these interactions (posts, comments, and upvotes) are stored in blocks on the blockchain, making them tamper-proof and visible to all network participants. This setup ensures that the data remains transparent, immutable, and secure, which is essential for maintaining trust and integrity in decentralized social platforms. Managing these interactions through a blockchain node helps ensure the platform operates without central control, promoting a fair and decentralized user experience.

As an operator, you will have control over the following:

Posts: Users on the platform can create posts, which are then validated and stored on the blockchain. You can configure how posts are handled, including setting up thresholds for posting rights and moderation.

Comments: Comments are also stored on the blockchain, and your node will validate each comment before it's published. You can configure whether comments need to be approved or can be automatically published.

Upvotes: Upvotes on content are tracked and stored in the blockchain. Your node may participate in validating these votes and ensuring that the rewards (tokens) are properly distributed based on the upvotes.

In decentralized platforms like Hive, nodes also play a role in content moderation and governance, so as a node operator, you may be involved in the decision-making process through community voting.

Building Your Own Social Media Blockchain

If you want to create your own decentralized social media platform from scratch, blockchain offers an excellent foundation. Here's how to design and build your own platform.

How to Start Your Own Decentralized Social Media Platform

Starting your own blockchain-based social media platform involves several key steps:

Choose a Consensus Mechanism: Decide whether your platform will use Proof of Work (PoW), Proof of Stake (PoS), or another consensus mechanism. PoW is more resource-intensive but secure, while PoS is energy-efficient and provides incentives for holding tokens.

Select Blockchain Infrastructure: Build the blockchain infrastructure from the ground up or fork an existing blockchain, such as Steemit or Hive. You'll need to decide on the technology stack, such as using Ethereum, EOS, or creating a custom blockchain.

Develop Smart Contracts: Develop smart contracts that define the rules of interaction on the platform. These smart contracts handle things like post creation, voting mechanisms, and cryptocurrency rewards.

Design the User Interface: The user interface (UI) is essential for making the platform user-friendly, providing an intuitive and seamless experience for users interacting with the system. While the platform itself is built on blockchain technology, the UI acts as the web interface that allows users to engage with the blockchain in a simple, accessible way.

The UI should allow users to easily post content, comment, upvote, and interact with other users in real-time, just like any traditional social platform. However, unlike conventional platforms, the actions users take (such as posting a message, commenting, or voting) are recorded and verified on the blockchain, ensuring transparency, security, and decentralization.

Key aspects of the UI design should include:

Simple Navigation: Clear and intuitive layouts that guide users through the process of posting content, interacting with other users, and navigating the platform. Users should not need to worry about the underlying blockchain mechanisms.

Blockchain Interaction: The UI should integrate seamlessly with the blockchain. For example, when a user submits a post or upvotes content, these actions trigger transactions that are recorded on the blockchain. The UI can show the user how their actions are verified and validated through blockchain processes, such as through confirmation messages or transaction IDs.

Real-Time Updates: The platform should provide real-time updates on posts, comments, and upvotes, reflecting the blockchain's decentralized nature. As interactions happen, the UI should dynamically update without requiring page reloads, offering a smooth user experience while the blockchain processes the data in the background.

Token Integration: If the platform uses cryptocurrency or tokens as part of its incentive system (such as rewarding users for posting or voting), the UI should allow users to easily view their balance, track transactions, and interact with the blockchain-based economy of the platform. This might include options for earning tokens, transferring tokens, or viewing token-related transactions.

The user interface acts as the bridge between the user and the blockchain, providing the tools for interacting with the blockchain in a way that is intuitive and user-friendly, while abstracting the complexity of the underlying decentralized system. The goal is to make the blockchain's advantages, such as security, transparency, and decentralization, accessible to users in a familiar web interface.

Create a Cryptocurrency: Integrate a cryptocurrency into the platform to incentivize users. This cryptocurrency can reward users for content creation, engagement, and other valuable actions on the platform. In the context of a barter system, cryptocurrency can also serve as the medium for exchanges, making it easier for users to trade goods and services directly. Additionally, you could set up a tokenomics model to reward both creators and curators of content, ensuring that participants are motivated to contribute to the platform's growth. By using cryptocurrency, even traditional barter systems can benefit from the efficiencies of digital currency, providing seamless transactions and reinforcing the platform's decentralized nature.

Designing the Infrastructure and Incentivizing Users with Cryptocurrency

Incentive Structure: Define how users will earn rewards for their contributions. For example, users might earn tokens for posting, commenting, and voting. These tokens can either be used within the platform (e.g., to purchase services) or exchanged for other cryptocurrencies.

Governance Mechanism: Implement a governance mechanism that allows users to vote on platform updates, content moderation policies, and other decisions. Token holders can vote on proposals, ensuring that the platform remains decentralized.

Privacy and Data Control: Ensure that your platform provides users with control over their data. Blockchain's immutability ensures that content remains permanently available, but it's crucial to implement encryption and privacy policies to protect user data.

Scalability: As your platform grows, it's important to design your blockchain to be scalable. This means ensuring it can handle a large number of posts, comments, and interactions without slowing down or becoming too expensive to use.

With blockchain, you can create a decentralized social media platform where users control their content, data, and interactions. This system encourages greater freedom, transparency, and fairness while offering users the ability to earn rewards for their contributions.

Chapter 7: Blockchain for Content Distribution

Decentralized Content Sharing

Content distribution has long been dominated by centralized platforms like YouTube, Spotify, and traditional file-sharing networks. These platforms act as intermediaries, controlling access to content and taking a large portion of the revenue generated. Blockchain technology offers a solution to decentralize content distribution, providing creators with more control over their work and allowing users to access content without the need for centralized services.

Why Decentralize Content Distribution? Benefits and Challenges

Benefits

Control and Ownership: With blockchain, content creators retain control over their intellectual property (IP). Instead of having their content hosted on centralized servers, creators can distribute their work directly to users through blockchain networks, reducing the risk of content censorship, unfair revenue sharing, or loss of access.

Monetization: Blockchain allows for direct transactions with audiences. By using smart contracts, creators can earn cryptocurrency for each view, download, or interaction. This eliminates the need for intermediaries who take a significant cut of the revenue.

Transparency: Blockchain enables transparent content tracking. Creators can monitor who is viewing or sharing their content, ensuring they are paid fairly for every transaction. Audiences also benefit from the transparency of blockchain, knowing that their interactions are secure and untraceable by third parties.

Security and Censorship Resistance: Blockchain's decentralized nature means there is no single point of failure. This reduces the risk of hacking, content removal, and censorship by centralized authorities.

Challenges

Scalability: As content distribution increases, blockchain networks must be able to handle the large amounts of data and transactions involved. Scaling decentralized systems to support millions of users without causing delays or high transaction fees is a technical challenge.

User Experience: Blockchain-based content platforms are still in their early stages, and the user experience often lags behind centralized platforms. Users must understand how cryptocurrency, wallets, and blockchain work, which can be a barrier to widespread adoption.

Adoption: Many users are accustomed to centralized platforms and may be reluctant to switch to decentralized alternatives, especially if those alternatives are less familiar or require additional technical knowledge.

Blockchain Platforms for Content Creators: Audius, Livepeer, and More

Many blockchain-based platforms are specifically designed to support content creators and disrupt traditional content distribution models.

Audius: Audius is a decentralized music streaming platform built on blockchain technology. It allows artists to upload their music directly and earn cryptocurrency for their streams, bypassing intermediaries like record labels and streaming services. Audius uses a token called AUDIO, which is used for governance, staking, and rewarding creators. By decentralizing music streaming, Audius enables musicians to retain control over their content and revenue.

Livepeer: Livepeer is a decentralized video streaming platform that allows users to stream video content without relying on centralized infrastructure. It uses blockchain technology to create an open, peer-to-peer network for video encoding and streaming. Livepeer enables content creators to broadcast video in a cost-effective manner and earn rewards through a native cryptocurrency, LPT (Livepeer Token).

Filecoin: Filecoin is a decentralized storage network that allows content creators to store and share files in a distributed manner. Creators can earn Filecoin tokens for renting out storage space on their devices. The network uses blockchain to ensure data integrity and prevent unauthorized access.

Arweave: Arweave is a decentralized storage network designed for long-term data storage. It uses blockchain technology to provide permanent, tamper-proof data storage, which is ideal for content creators who need to preserve research, data sets, and scientific publications. Arweave enables users to pay once to store content forever, ensuring the permanence and availability of scientific data or educational resources.

IPFS (InterPlanetary File System): IPFS is a peer-to-peer file storage and sharing network that enables decentralized file storage across the world. It's often used in conjunction with blockchain technology to ensure that content is accessible without relying on centralized servers. For content creators in science and research, IPFS can be used to share large datasets, research papers, or other scientific documents securely and transparently.

DTube: DTube is a decentralized video-sharing platform built on the Steemit blockchain. It operates similarly to YouTube but allows creators to upload videos and earn cryptocurrency through the platform's token economy. DTube provides a censorship-resistant environment, making it an attractive choice for content creators in scientific and educational fields who want to share videos without fear of de-platforming.

PublishOx: PublishOx is a blockchain-based publishing platform that rewards both content creators and readers with cryptocurrency. It is designed to allow writers, journalists, and creators to earn through a decentralized model. The platform uses Ethereum and the PublishOx token (POX) for content creation, curation, and tipping. Scientific authors or educators can publish articles or research findings and directly earn tokens from readers' engagement.

Ocean Protocol: Ocean Protocol is a decentralized data exchange protocol that enables content creators in the data and research fields to share and monetize their data. It allows data owners (such as scientific researchers) to maintain control over their data while allowing buyers to access and utilize it for analysis or research. Ocean Protocol uses blockchain to ensure data privacy and secure transactions, promoting transparency and trust in scientific data sharing.

Creative Commons on Blockchain: Platforms like *CreativeCoin* are built on blockchain technology and allow content creators to publish and share their work using Creative Commons licenses. This decentralized approach helps creators maintain control over the licensing and distribution of their work while benefiting from the security and transparency of blockchain technology.

Po.et: Po.et is a blockchain-based platform for content creators to register, timestamp, and protect their digital works, such as articles, music, and research papers. By utilizing blockchain, Po.et helps ensure the authenticity, ownership, and licensing of creative and scientific works. Researchers, writers, and journalists can use Po.et to claim ownership and protect their intellectual property in a secure and transparent manner.

Contentos: Contentos is a decentralized content ecosystem that connects creators, advertisers, and users through a blockchain-powered platform. It allows creators to earn tokens through the production and sharing of content. Contentos is used for both entertainment and educational content, and its blockchain technology ensures that creators are rewarded fairly for their work, while enabling a more transparent system for all parties involved.

Decentraland: Though primarily a virtual world and metaverse platform, Decentraland is built on blockchain and allows content creators to build, monetize, and share their virtual worlds and experiences. For science-related content creators, Decentraland could be used for creating immersive educational content, virtual museums, or exhibitions that provide a new way for users to engage with scientific knowledge.

Zora: Zora is a decentralized marketplace built on Ethereum, primarily for creators of digital art. However, it can also be applied to scientific and academic content creators, as it allows for the creation of digital assets that can be bought, sold, or traded. Researchers and educators can tokenize their work (such as journal articles, research papers, and datasets) and sell access to their knowledge or data in a transparent, blockchain-based marketplace.

These platforms are examples of how blockchain can disrupt traditional content-sharing models, enabling creators to distribute their work securely and directly to audiences.

Setting Up a Content Distribution Node

Running a node for decentralized content distribution allows you to participate in the sharing and validation of content. Nodes can be set up for various types of decentralized platforms, including music, video, and file sharing.

Running a Node for Decentralized Video, Music, or File Sharing

Running a content distribution node typically involves hosting data on a peer-to-peer network where you store, share, or stream content. This process may vary depending on the platform you're using.

For instance, in Audius, nodes are run by a network of providers who offer storage and bandwidth for music streaming. Similarly, in Livepeer, nodes can encode and distribute live video streams.

Steps for Setting Up a Content Distribution Node:

Choose a Platform: Select the content-sharing platform you want to support (e.g., Audius, Livepeer, or Filecoin).

Install Node Software: Each platform requires specific software to run a node. For instance, for Audius, you may need to install and configure their software, which often requires running a server on a machine with sufficient processing power and bandwidth.

Synchronize the Blockchain: As with any blockchain network, your node will need to sync with the rest of the network. This may involve downloading large amounts of data and ensuring that your node is fully updated before it can participate.

Provide Storage or Encoding: Depending on the platform, your node will either store content (in the case of Filecoin) or encode and distribute video (in the case of Livepeer). You may need to allocate sufficient resources on your server, such as disk space for file storage or bandwidth for streaming.

Earn Rewards: Many platforms reward node operators with cryptocurrency for their contributions. This could include payment for providing bandwidth, storage, or encoding power. By running a node, you're helping to ensure that the content is distributed in a decentralized manner.

How to Manage and Share Content Securely on the Blockchain

Data Encryption: It's important to encrypt sensitive content before uploading it to the blockchain. Many platforms support encrypted file storage, which ensures that only authorized users can access or decrypt the content.

Smart Contracts: Use smart contracts to manage the terms of content distribution. For example, a smart contract could automate the distribution of rewards based on the number of views a video gets, or it could manage access permissions for private content.

Content Integrity: Blockchain ensures that once content is uploaded, it cannot be altered or tampered with. The blockchain serves as a transparent ledger that tracks who uploads, views, and shares content, offering a high degree of security and trust.

Privacy Considerations: While blockchain offers secure and transparent data storage, it's important to be mindful of user privacy. Some blockchain platforms allow creators to make content private or share it only with specific audiences, while others may be entirely open.

Building a Content Distribution Network (CDN)

Traditional CDNs are centralized networks of servers designed to deliver content quickly to users by caching content on geographically distributed servers. While effective, they are subject to issues such as single points of failure, centralized control, and high costs for scaling. Blockchain technology offers the potential to decentralize and disrupt the CDN model, providing more reliable, cost-effective, and censorship-resistant alternatives.

How Blockchain Technology Can Disrupt Traditional CDN Models

Blockchain technology has the potential to disrupt traditional Content Delivery Networks (CDNs) by decentralizing content storage and distribution, reducing reliance on centralized infrastructure. Unlike traditional CDNs, which depend on centralized servers vulnerable to single points of failure, blockchain enables content to be fragmented, encrypted, and distributed across a decentralized network of nodes. This enhances security, reduces the risk of disruptions from attacks or server overloads, and improves content delivery speed, especially in remote areas. Blockchain's peer-to-peer architecture also cuts costs by eliminating intermediaries and allowing for more efficient, transparent content tracking and payments through smart contracts. Additionally, it gives creators more control over their intellectual property and ensures data privacy for users. Overall, blockchain can create a more resilient, cost-effective, and scalable content delivery system that benefits both content creators and consumers while fostering greater security, transparency, and decentralization.

Some of the ways blockchain can disrupt traditional CDN models include:

Cost Reduction: With blockchain-based CDNs, content can be distributed using a peer-to-peer network. This reduces the need for expensive infrastructure, such as data centers and CDN providers.

Scalability: Blockchain-based CDNs are inherently more scalable. As more users participate in the network by providing storage and bandwidth, the capacity of the CDN naturally grows.

Fault Tolerance: Decentralized content delivery is more resistant to failure because content is distributed across many nodes, making it less vulnerable to server outages or attacks.

Security and Privacy: Blockchain-based CDNs use encryption to ensure that content is stored and transmitted securely. In addition, by decentralizing control, blockchain reduces the likelihood of content censorship or manipulation.

Running a Blockchain-Powered CDN on Your Own Server

Running your own blockchain-powered CDN involves using blockchain to distribute and deliver content across a network of nodes.

The basic steps include:

Set Up a Blockchain Node: Install the necessary software for the blockchain CDN you wish to use. For instance, if you are setting up your own decentralized video streaming network, you could use a protocol like Livepeer.

Allocate Storage and Bandwidth: Provide resources for content storage and distribution. This includes setting up large amounts of disk space for storing videos, music, or files, as well as ensuring you have sufficient bandwidth to serve content to users.

Join the Network: Once your node is configured, join the decentralized network of nodes that distribute content. Depending on the platform, your node may become part of a larger decentralized CDN that serves content to users in a more efficient and cost-effective manner.

Monitor and Maintain Your Node: Like any blockchain node, it's important to regularly monitor and maintain your CDN node. Ensure that it's syncing with the network, updating to the latest version of the blockchain, and providing content efficiently to users.

By utilizing blockchain for content distribution, you can create a more democratic, secure, and cost-effective content delivery network. Running a blockchain-powered CDN can provide both personal and professional opportunities, whether you're sharing personal content or distributing media at scale.

Chapter 8: Blockchain for Decentralized Finance (DeFi)

Introduction to DeFi

Decentralized Finance (DeFi) is a rapidly growing sector within the blockchain and cryptocurrency ecosystem. DeFi aims to replicate traditional financial services—such as lending, borrowing, trading, and investing—through decentralized networks, using smart contracts and blockchain technology. Unlike traditional finance, which relies on intermediaries such as banks, brokers, and insurance companies, DeFi platforms operate on public blockchains like Ethereum, enabling peer-to-peer transactions without the need for central authorities.

What is Decentralized Finance (DeFi) and How Does It Work?

Decentralized Finance (DeFi) uses blockchain technology and smart contracts to offer financial services without relying on traditional intermediaries like banks. Built mostly on blockchain networks like Ethereum, DeFi platforms allow users to access products such as lending, borrowing, trading, and insurance. These services operate through smart contracts, which automatically execute transactions based on predefined conditions, reducing costs, increasing transparency, and making the process more efficient. By removing intermediaries, DeFi aims to democratize access to financial services and improve financial inclusion.

A key benefit of DeFi is its openness, allowing anyone with an internet connection to participate, regardless of location or financial background. DeFi platforms are often governed by decentralized autonomous organizations (DAOs), where users can vote on protocol changes and upgrades. Despite its advantages, DeFi carries risks, including smart contract vulnerabilities, market volatility, and regulatory uncertainty. However, the DeFi ecosystem continues to grow, with innovations like yield farming, staking, and decentralized insurance pointing to the potential for a more inclusive financial system.

Blockchain Infrastructure: DeFi platforms are built on public blockchains like Ethereum, Binance Smart Chain (BSC), or Avalanche. These blockchains allow users to execute transactions directly on the network using smart contracts—automated programs that execute predefined actions when certain conditions are met.

Smart Contracts: Smart contracts are self-executing contracts with the terms of the agreement directly written into lines of code. These contracts automate financial transactions such as lending, borrowing, and trading, without the need for intermediaries.

Cryptocurrency as Collateral: In DeFi, users can provide cryptocurrency as collateral to borrow funds, or they can lend their cryptocurrency to earn interest. Transactions are executed through smart contracts that ensure transparency and trust in the process.

Liquidity Pools: Liquidity is provided to platforms through liquidity pools, where users deposit their tokens and earn rewards in return, typically in the form of transaction fees or tokens. This is a cornerstone of many DeFi protocols.

Key DeFi Platforms: Uniswap, Aave, Compound, etc.

Several DeFi platforms have become popular in recent years, each offering unique services and opportunities for users to engage with decentralized finance.

Uniswap: Uniswap is a decentralized exchange (DEX) that allows users to trade ERC-20 tokens directly from their wallets without the need for a central intermediary. It uses an automated market maker (AMM) model, where liquidity is provided by users, and trades are executed through smart contracts.

Aave: Aave is a decentralized lending platform that allows users to lend and borrow a variety of cryptocurrencies. Users can earn interest by lending their assets to liquidity pools or take out loans by collateralizing their crypto holdings.

Compound: Compound is another decentralized lending protocol, but it enables users to earn interest on their cryptocurrencies by lending them to liquidity pools. Users can also borrow from the pool by offering collateral in the form of other cryptocurrencies.

These platforms rely on decentralized governance and transparent smart contracts, where the rules and operations are open to public verification.

The Role of Blockchain Nodes in DeFi Systems

Blockchain nodes are the backbone of DeFi platforms. Nodes in DeFi networks perform several critical functions:

Transaction Verification: Nodes validate transactions within the network, ensuring that each transaction meets the required consensus rules of the blockchain.

Smart Contract Execution: Nodes are responsible for executing the smart contracts that power DeFi applications. When a user interacts with a DeFi platform, the node executes the code behind the transaction to ensure the correct outcome.

Data Availability: Nodes maintain and update the blockchain ledger, making sure that data related to DeFi protocols—such as transaction histories, collateral, and loan balances—is securely stored and accessible to all participants in the network.

Running your own node gives you greater autonomy in interacting with DeFi platforms, as it reduces reliance on third-party services while enhancing privacy and security.

Setting Up a DeFi Node

Setting up a DeFi node allows you to interact directly with decentralized financial networks, giving you more control and autonomy over your assets and transactions. DeFi nodes act as a bridge between your local environment and the decentralized platform, enabling you to access services like lending, borrowing, staking, and trading without relying on third-party intermediaries. By running your own node, you can validate transactions, access data in real-time, and have more secure and direct access to decentralized exchanges (DEXs) and other DeFi protocols.

To set up a DeFi node, you'll typically need to install the necessary blockchain client software, such as the Ethereum client (like Geth or OpenEthereum) for Ethereum-based DeFi platforms. This requires adequate hardware resources, including sufficient storage, CPU, and internet bandwidth to keep the node synchronized with the blockchain. Once your node is running, you can participate in governance, earn rewards through staking, and maintain full control over your wallet and assets. Additionally, running a node enhances the decentralization of the network, supporting its growth and security.

Running a Node to Interact with Decentralized Finance Platforms

To run a DeFi node, you'll need to set up a blockchain node for the network where the DeFi platform operates (e.g., Ethereum, Binance Smart Chain, or other blockchain platforms).

Choose a Blockchain Network: Select the blockchain network that hosts the DeFi platform you want to use (such as Ethereum for Uniswap or Compound).

Install Node Software: Download and install the relevant node software (e.g., Geth for Ethereum, BSC Node for Binance Smart Chain). Running a full node involves syncing with the blockchain, which may take a considerable amount of storage space and time.

Configure the Node: Once the node software is installed, configure it to interact with the DeFi protocols you're interested in. You might need to connect your node to decentralized applications (dApps) through a Web3 interface like Metamask or WalletConnect.

Synchronize the Blockchain: After configuring the node, it will begin syncing with the blockchain network. This may take some time, depending on the blockchain's size and the speed of your internet connection.

Interact with DeFi Platforms: Once your node is fully synchronized, you can interact with DeFi platforms directly through smart contracts. This could include participating in decentralized lending, trading, or providing liquidity.

How to Stake Cryptocurrency or Provide Liquidity to DeFi Protocols

Staking cryptocurrency and providing liquidity to DeFi protocols are two common ways to earn rewards within decentralized finance. Staking involves locking up a certain amount of cryptocurrency in a DeFi platform or blockchain network to support operations like transaction validation or network security. In return, stakers receive rewards, often in the form of the staked token or additional cryptocurrency. Providing liquidity, on the other hand, involves depositing cryptocurrency into a liquidity pool on decentralized exchanges (DEXs) to facilitate trading. In exchange for supplying liquidity, users earn a share of the transaction fees or rewards generated by the platform. Both methods allow participants to earn passive income, though they come with risks such as price volatility, smart contract vulnerabilities, and potential impermanent loss, particularly in liquidity provision.

Staking and liquidity provision are two ways to earn rewards in DeFi systems. Here's how you can get started:

Staking: Staking involves locking up a certain amount of cryptocurrency in a smart contract to support the network (e.g., validating transactions or securing the network). In return, you earn rewards, often in the form of additional cryptocurrency. For example, Ethereum 2.0 staking allows users to stake ETH and earn rewards for validating transactions.

Steps to Stake:

Choose a staking platform (e.g., Ethereum 2.0 staking, Aave, or Compound).

Deposit the cryptocurrency you wish to stake into the staking contract.

Monitor your staking rewards periodically and claim them when possible.

Providing Liquidity: By providing liquidity to a platform like Uniswap or Compound, you are contributing tokens to liquidity pools. In exchange, you earn transaction fees or governance tokens. The more liquidity you provide, the higher your potential rewards.

Steps to Provide Liquidity:
Choose a DeFi platform (e.g., Uniswap or Aave).

Deposit tokens into a liquidity pool.

Monitor your liquidity provider rewards and reinvest or claim them.

Earning Rewards from DeFi Networks

The rewards you earn from staking or providing liquidity depend on several factors, including the amount you stake or the liquidity you provide, the platform's transaction volume, and the network's overall activity. Some platforms, like Aave and Compound, also allow users to earn governance tokens, which can be used to vote on protocol changes.

Security and Risks in DeFi

While DeFi offers substantial opportunities for earning rewards and interacting with decentralized financial systems, it also carries risks that users must understand and mitigate.

How to Secure Your DeFi Investments

Securing your DeFi investments is vital because, unlike traditional financial systems, decentralized finance (DeFi) platforms operate without a central authority or intermediary to recover funds in the event of a security breach, error, or hack. One of the primary ways to secure your DeFi investments is by using hardware wallets, which store your private keys offline, providing a strong defense against online threats such as phishing and malware attacks. Additionally, enabling two-factor authentication (2FA) on your DeFi accounts can add an extra layer of protection, ensuring that even if your password is compromised, unauthorized access is still blocked. It's also essential to perform thorough due diligence before interacting with a DeFi platform, ensuring it is audited by reputable third parties and has a strong track record of security. You should also be cautious about the smart contracts you interact with, as vulnerabilities in these contracts can be exploited, potentially leading to the loss of your funds. Engaging with DeFi platforms that use insurance or protection mechanisms can help mitigate some risks, though no platform is completely risk-free. Finally, staying informed about the latest security practices and threats in the DeFi space, such as being aware of common scams, phishing attempts, and vulnerabilities, can help you make better decisions and safeguard your investments.

Here are a few security best practices:

Use Hardware Wallets: For better security, store your private keys and cryptocurrency in a hardware wallet, which is less susceptible to hacking than software wallets.

Double-check Smart Contracts: Before interacting with any DeFi platform, ensure that the platform's smart contracts have been audited and are free of vulnerabilities. DeFi platforms often undergo external audits to ensure their contracts are secure.

Use Multi-Factor Authentication: Many DeFi platforms and wallet providers offer multi-factor authentication (MFA) for an added layer of security. This can help protect your accounts from unauthorized access.

Backup Private Keys and Recovery Phrases: Always back up your private keys and recovery phrases in a secure, offline location. Losing access to your private key means losing access to your funds.

Risks Associated with DeFi Platforms and How to Mitigate Them

Smart Contract Bugs: DeFi protocols rely on smart contracts, and if a contract contains a bug, it can lead to the loss of funds or other vulnerabilities. Mitigate this risk by using well-established, audited platforms and avoiding platforms with no audits.

Impermanent Loss: Providing liquidity to decentralized exchanges (DEXs) can result in impermanent loss, which occurs when the value of your deposited tokens fluctuates compared to when they were initially added to the pool. To mitigate this, only provide liquidity to stablecoin pairs or low-volatility assets.

Platform Risk: Some DeFi platforms may be more prone to hacking or rug pulls (scams where developers withdraw funds from a project). Research platforms thoroughly, avoid platforms with low liquidity, and consider diversifying your investments.

Regulatory Uncertainty: The regulatory landscape for DeFi is still evolving, and changes in government policies may impact the legality or operation of certain DeFi protocols. Stay informed about potential regulatory developments.

By understanding the risks and taking appropriate security measures, you can safely participate in DeFi and leverage the benefits it offers.

Chapter 9: Optimizing and Scaling Your Blockchain Node

Performance Tuning

Blockchain nodes require significant computational power and resources, particularly when interacting with decentralized networks. Optimizing your blockchain node ensures that it runs efficiently, provides reliable access to the blockchain, and delivers optimal performance for transactions, data storage, and interaction with decentralized applications (dApps).

Optimizing Your Linux Server for Blockchain Operations

Linux is the most widely used operating system for running blockchain nodes due to its stability, performance, and flexibility.

To optimize a Linux server for blockchain operations, consider the following steps:

Use a Lightweight Distribution: Choose a minimal Linux distribution, like Ubuntu Server or Debian, which consume fewer resources and can be tailored to your blockchain node's needs. Avoid resource-heavy desktop environments or unnecessary services.

Disable Unused Services: Block unused services and processes to free up system resources. Tools like systemctl and htop can help identify unnecessary services that may be using CPU or memory.

Ensure Sufficient Virtual Memory (Swap): Although blockchain nodes heavily rely on RAM, it's good practice to configure an appropriate swap space on your server. Swap will serve as virtual memory, ensuring stability during periods of high demand.

Optimize the Disk I/O: Blockchain nodes require substantial disk I/O for logging and transaction processing. SSDs are preferred over HDDs due to their faster read/write speeds, reducing lag during synchronization and block validation.

Overclocking: In cases where your hardware allows, overclocking can boost CPU performance. However, this should be done carefully and within the manufacturer's guidelines to avoid overheating or hardware damage.

How to Allocate Resources Effectively (CPU, Memory, Storage)

Optimizing your server's resources is crucial to maintaining a responsive and fast blockchain node.

Here's how to allocate resources effectively:

CPU: Blockchain nodes require significant processing power, especially when validating transactions or running consensus algorithms (like Proof-of-Work or Proof-of-Stake). To optimize CPU usage:

Monitor CPU load: Use tools like htop or top to monitor your node's CPU usage.

Use multiple CPU cores: If your server has multiple cores, blockchain software often benefits from parallel processing. Ensure that your blockchain node is configured to utilize all available CPU cores effectively.

Memory: A blockchain node needs adequate memory to store the blockchain data and maintain smooth operation. The more memory your server has, the better it can handle heavy load and large datasets.

Monitor memory usage: Track memory usage with tools like free -h or vmstat to see if your node is running low on RAM.

Configure your node's memory requirements: Some blockchain nodes allow you to set memory limits or adjust parameters related to transaction processing or peer connections.

Storage: Blockchain data grows rapidly, so using high-performance storage is essential:

Use SSDs: Solid-State Drives (SSDs) offer faster read/write speeds, essential for maintaining a quick blockchain sync process.

Regularly clean the disk: Remove unnecessary files, logs, and data that are no longer needed. Blockchain nodes often produce large log files, so configure automatic log rotation to manage them.

By actively monitoring and managing these system resources, you can ensure your blockchain node runs optimally, minimizing downtime and performance bottlenecks.

Scaling Your Node for High Traffic

As blockchain networks grow in popularity, their transaction volume and data load increase, requiring a robust infrastructure to handle the traffic. Scaling your blockchain node is necessary to ensure it can handle high-demand periods without slowing down or crashing.

Running Multiple Blockchain Nodes on a Single Server

Running multiple blockchain nodes on a single server is an effective strategy for handling more than one blockchain network, especially if you need to interact with various blockchain ecosystems.

Here's how to do it efficiently:

Use Separate Directories for Each Node: When running multiple nodes, allocate a separate directory for each one to store their respective data and configuration files. This avoids conflicts and ensures that each node's operations are isolated.

CPU and Memory Allocation: To avoid resource contention, allocate a fixed amount of CPU and memory for each blockchain node. This can be done through resource management tools like cgroups or systemd on Linux.

Networking Configuration: Configure the firewall, network interfaces, and port forwarding to ensure that each node has a dedicated port for communication with the blockchain network.

Running multiple nodes on a single server helps maximize hardware utilization, but it is crucial to monitor resource usage to avoid overloading the system.

Using Docker or Virtualization to Isolate Different Blockchain Networks

Containerization and virtualization technologies like Docker or VirtualBox provide an efficient and scalable way to run blockchain nodes while isolating them from each other and the host system. This approach allows for greater flexibility and resource management.

Docker: Docker enables you to run multiple blockchain nodes in isolated containers on a single server. Each container has its own environment, dependencies, and file system.

Benefits of Docker:

Easy setup: With pre-configured Docker images for popular blockchains like Ethereum or Bitcoin, setting up a node is straightforward.

Resource efficiency: Docker containers are lightweight, offering high resource efficiency compared to virtual machines.

Isolation: Docker allows you to isolate nodes for different blockchain networks, preventing interference and reducing the risk of conflicts.

Setting up a Dockerized Blockchain Node:

Install Docker on your Linux server.

Pull a Docker image for the blockchain node you want to run (e.g., ethereum/client-go for Ethereum).

Configure the container's resource limits and network settings.

Start the container and monitor performance using Docker's built-in monitoring tools.

Virtualization: Virtualization allows you to run multiple full-fledged virtual machines (VMs), each hosting its own blockchain node.

Benefits of Virtualization:

Complete Isolation: Virtual machines provide stronger isolation than containers, making them ideal for security-sensitive applications.

Full Operating Systems: Each VM can run a full operating system, providing more flexibility in terms of node configuration and resource allocation.

Setting up a Virtualized Blockchain Node:

Install a virtualization tool like VirtualBox or KVM on your server.

Create virtual machines for each blockchain node you want to run.

Allocate resources (CPU, memory, and storage) for each VM according to the node's needs.

Install the required blockchain software on each VM and configure it to connect to the appropriate network.

Improving Node Synchronization Speed

When first setting up a blockchain node, the synchronization process—downloading the entire blockchain history and verifying all transactions—can be time-consuming and resource-intensive. Improving the synchronization speed can make it easier to set up new nodes or recover from downtime.

Techniques to Speed Up the Initial Synchronization of the Blockchain

Several strategies can help you speed up the initial synchronization process:

Use Fast Sync or Light Sync: Many blockchain networks offer a "fast sync" mode, which downloads only the latest state of the blockchain (instead of the entire history) and verifies it. This can significantly reduce the time required to sync.

Peer-to-Peer Connection Optimization: By configuring your node to connect to high-performance, well-connected peers (often known as "bootnodes"), you can speed up the synchronization process.

Find High-Quality Peers: Use peer discovery features of the node software or join community-run node lists to find high-performance peers.

Upgrade Hardware: Faster CPUs, more memory, and faster SSDs can reduce synchronization time. Investing in hardware that meets the recommended specifications for running blockchain nodes can make a notable difference.

How to Prune the Blockchain or Use Light Nodes for Faster Operation

Pruning: Some blockchains allow you to "prune" the blockchain, meaning that old or unnecessary blocks (such as those that are no longer needed for transaction verification) are deleted to save space. While this reduces disk space usage, it may limit the ability to validate the full transaction history.

Light Nodes: Light nodes (or SPV nodes) only download the necessary parts of the blockchain, such as block headers and transaction metadata, instead of the entire blockchain. This results in much faster synchronization and lower resource requirements, but it sacrifices some degree of decentralization and trust.

Optimize Synchronization Settings: Some blockchain software allows you to tweak synchronization parameters, such as the number of concurrent connections to peers or the block validation depth. Adjusting these settings can speed up synchronization.

Chapter 10: Maintaining and Monitoring Your Blockchain Server

Regular Maintenance

Maintaining a blockchain node involves more than just ensuring that the node is running. Regular updates, security patches, and optimizations are essential to keep your server performing at its best while ensuring it remains secure from attacks or vulnerabilities.

Updating and Securing Your Blockchain Software

Regularly updating your blockchain software is one of the most important tasks to ensure your server remains secure and compatible with the latest network changes. This includes both the blockchain node software itself and any dependencies it might have.

Software Updates:
Keep your blockchain node software up to date to benefit from security patches, new features, and network upgrades (e.g., hard forks, protocol changes). Most blockchain networks release new versions regularly to address bugs and

vulnerabilities.

For Linux systems, use package management tools like apt, yum, or dnf to ensure that system dependencies are also up to date.

Security Patches:
Security vulnerabilities can expose your server to attacks such as denial-of-service (DoS) or unauthorized access. Regularly check for and install security updates for both your blockchain software and the underlying Linux server operating system.

Subscribe to security mailing lists for the specific blockchain project to get timely information on new security patches or vulnerabilities.

System Hardening:
Implement general Linux security best practices, such as disabling unnecessary services, configuring firewalls (e.g., ufw or iptables), and using strong authentication methods (e.g., SSH key-based login instead of password-based login).

Set up a VPN or other secure tunneling protocol for remote access to your blockchain node. This ensures that any external connection is encrypted and protected from potential eavesdropping.

How to Keep Your Linux Server Secure and Efficient Over Time

Over time, the efficiency and security of your server can degrade due to configuration changes, software bloat, or emerging threats.

Here are some steps to keep your Linux server secure and running efficiently:

Regular Backups: Back up the blockchain data and configuration files at regular intervals. This will protect your server from potential data loss due to hardware failure or other issues.

Use automated backup tools (e.g., rsync, cron jobs) to create regular backups of critical files and blockchain data.

Resource Management: As your blockchain node operates, its resource consumption (CPU, memory, storage) can grow. Use tools like top, htop, iotop, and df to monitor resource usage over time. Adjust resource allocation or add hardware as necessary.

Set up alerts for high resource usage (e.g., CPU spikes or disk usage nearing capacity).

Regular Disk Cleanup: Blockchain nodes can generate large log files and cache that may not be necessary after a certain period. Use tools like logrotate to manage logs or manually clear old logs and temporary files periodically.

Regularly prune the blockchain data (if supported by your blockchain) to reduce storage requirements.

System Audits: Periodically perform system audits to ensure there are no unnecessary or outdated processes consuming resources. This also helps identify security gaps and potential weaknesses in your configuration.

Tools like Lynis and OpenVAS can automate security audits on your Linux server.

Monitoring Node Health

Blockchain nodes can become unresponsive or inefficient without proper monitoring. Setting up real-time monitoring tools allows you to proactively address issues before they disrupt the node's operation.

Setting Up Monitoring Tools to Track the Performance and Health of Your Node

Monitoring your blockchain node's performance is essential for ensuring it remains healthy and performs optimally.

There are several tools and practices you can employ:

System Monitoring Tools:

Prometheus and Grafana: Use Prometheus to collect performance metrics from your blockchain node, including CPU usage, memory consumption, disk I/O, and network activity. Grafana can visualize these metrics in a dashboard for real-time monitoring.

Netdata: A lightweight, real-time monitoring tool that provides detailed insights into server performance, including resource usage, network activity, and hardware statistics.

Nagios: A powerful, customizable monitoring tool for ensuring that your blockchain node and server are running smoothly. Nagios can be configured to track various metrics and services, alerting you if something goes wrong.

Blockchain-Specific Monitoring:
Many blockchain networks provide their own monitoring solutions or third-party tools tailored to track node performance, such as block sync status, peer count, transaction volume, etc.

Tools like Blockchair (for Bitcoin and other networks) and Etherscan (for Ethereum) provide block explorers with additional metrics and health checks, including the status of individual nodes.

Using Alerts to Ensure Your Node Stays Online and Synchronized

Alerts are crucial for quickly identifying issues such as downtime, high resource consumption, or syncing problems.

Set up monitoring tools to trigger alerts under specific conditions:

Resource Usage Alerts: Set up alerts for high CPU, memory, or disk usage. For example, if CPU usage exceeds a threshold for more than a specified time, you can be alerted.

Syncing Alerts: If your node falls out of sync with the blockchain, it can miss important transactions or blocks. Set up alerts to notify you when the node falls behind in syncing, or if the synchronization process fails completely.

Network Connectivity Alerts: Blockchain nodes rely heavily on stable internet connections to communicate with the rest of the network. Alerts should notify you of network issues, high latency, or dropped connections.

Service Uptime Monitoring: Use services like UptimeRobot or Pingdom to monitor your node's availability from multiple locations around the world. These services can alert you if your node goes offline.

Troubleshooting Common Issues

Blockchain nodes can experience various issues that may disrupt their functionality. Common problems include syncing issues, network connectivity problems, and resource bottlenecks. Knowing how to troubleshoot these problems is essential to maintaining uptime and reliability.

Identifying and Fixing Common Blockchain Node Problems

Here are some common issues you might encounter and how to resolve them:

Syncing Issues: If your node is stuck or failing to sync with the blockchain, try the following steps:

Check Network Connectivity: Ensure that your server has a stable internet connection and can connect to the blockchain network's peers. You can use tools like ping, traceroute, or curl to test the connection to known blockchain nodes.

Verify Node Version Compatibility: Ensure that your node is running the correct version of the blockchain software. Sometimes network upgrades (forks) may require you to update your node software to remain compatible with the rest of the network.

Restart the Node: If syncing issues persist, restart your blockchain node and check if it resumes syncing properly. Sometimes, a fresh start can resolve stuck or stuck transactions.

Network Connectivity Problems: If your node is having trouble connecting to peers or experiencing high latency, the issue could lie in network configuration.

Check Firewall Settings: Ensure that your firewall is not blocking the necessary ports for blockchain communication. Each blockchain network has specific ports that must remain open (e.g., Bitcoin uses port 8333).

Peer Discovery: If your node cannot find peers, try manually adding known peers using their IP addresses or peer lists. Some blockchains have community-maintained lists of trusted peers.

Debugging Syncing Issues and Network Connectivity Problems

Examine Logs: Always check the logs of your blockchain node to diagnose issues. Logs often contain detailed error messages that can point you toward the problem. Look for error messages related to synchronization, block validation, or peer connections.

Use journalctl (for systemd-based services) or check the log files in /var/log/ to see what's happening in the background.

Use Debugging Tools: Some blockchain nodes provide built-in debugging tools or commands that can help identify specific issues. For example, the geth (Go Ethereum) command-line tool provides various debugging flags to help track down syncing or networking issues.

Check Blockchain Network Status: It's also important to check the health of the blockchain network itself. Use block explorers or community forums to verify if there are any known issues, such as a network split or congestion.

Future Developments

What's Next

Blockchain technology is still in its early stages, but its potential to disrupt traditional industries and create new decentralized solutions is immense. As blockchain networks evolve, so do the opportunities for expanding the use cases of your blockchain node setup. Understanding where blockchain technology is heading and how you can be a part of its future development is crucial to staying ahead of the curve.

Expanding Your Blockchain Node Setup for Other Use Cases

While many blockchain nodes are primarily used for cryptocurrencies or decentralized finance (DeFi), the technology behind these nodes can be leveraged for a variety of new and emerging use cases.

Here are some potential areas where you can expand your blockchain node setup:

Decentralized Identity (DID):
Blockchain nodes are being utilized to build decentralized

identity systems that allow individuals to control their own identities without relying on central authorities like governments or corporations. You can integrate your node into a decentralized identity network, helping to authenticate users securely and privately.

Solutions like Sovrin and uPort are at the forefront of decentralized identity, and blockchain nodes could play a key role in verifying and validating identities on these platforms.

Supply Chain Management:
Blockchain technology is being increasingly used to track goods along supply chains in a transparent, immutable manner. Your node could be part of a network that logs every step of a product's journey, from manufacturing to delivery.

Popular platforms like VeChain and IBM Food Trust utilize blockchain nodes to ensure authenticity, traceability, and transparency within supply chains. Integrating these types of nodes into your setup could open doors to various industries, from food safety to luxury goods verification.

Decentralized Web (Web 3.0):
As we transition to Web 3.0, a new era of the internet built on decentralized networks, your blockchain node could become part of the infrastructure for hosting decentralized websites, applications, and content. This new internet would run on peer-to-peer networks instead of traditional client-server models.

Blockchain platforms like **IPFS** (InterPlanetary File System) and Filecoin allow decentralized storage and sharing of files, while Ethereum and Polkadot provide frameworks for decentralized applications (dApps). Running a node on these platforms could give you access to the future of the internet.

Digital Rights Management (DRM):
With the increasing need to manage and protect digital assets, blockchain can be used to create decentralized systems for copyright enforcement, licensing, and distribution of content. A blockchain node could help verify ownership and prevent piracy, ensuring that content creators are compensated fairly for their work.

Blockchain-based projects like Audius (for music) and KodakOne (for photography) are already exploring DRM solutions that leverage blockchain's transparency and immutability.

Decentralized Storage:
Blockchain can facilitate the development of decentralized storage solutions where data is distributed across multiple nodes rather than relying on centralized cloud providers. Your blockchain node could help to store encrypted files on the network, making it more secure and resistant to censorship.

Examples include Storj, Filecoin, and Arweave, which are decentralized storage platforms utilizing blockchain nodes for distributed data storage. This provides an alternative to traditional cloud services like Google Drive and Dropbox.

Blockchain for IoT (Internet of Things):

Blockchain nodes can also be integrated into Internet of Things (IoT) ecosystems, enabling secure, automated, and decentralized communication between connected devices. With the rise of smart homes, connected cars, and industrial IoT, your node can help facilitate seamless data exchange and device management.

Platforms like IOTA and Helium are working towards building decentralized IoT networks, where blockchain nodes manage and validate communication between devices, offering security, scalability, and reliability.

Continuing to Explore the Potential of Decentralized Technologies

Blockchain is not an isolated technology. It often intersects with other innovative decentralized technologies that are shaping the future. Continuing to explore these technologies will give you a broader understanding of the opportunities that lie ahead.

Decentralized Autonomous Organizations (DAOs):
DAOs are organizations governed by smart contracts, allowing decentralized decision-making and voting. As blockchain technologies evolve, the role of DAOs will become increasingly important in sectors such as governance, community projects, and business operations.

Running a node within a DAO framework could enable you to participate in the governance of a decentralized organization, influencing decisions about the direction of projects, fund allocations, and more.

Interoperability between Blockchains:
One of the key challenges facing blockchain technology is the lack of interoperability between different blockchain networks. Cross-chain communication solutions are under development, allowing assets and data to flow freely between blockchains, enabling more collaboration and utility across different ecosystems.

Projects like Polkadot and Cosmos are working on blockchain interoperability. Running nodes within these ecosystems could make your infrastructure a crucial part of the interconnected blockchain world.

Quantum Computing and Blockchain:
As quantum computing technology matures, it poses both challenges and opportunities for blockchain. While quantum computers could theoretically break the cryptography used in most blockchain systems, blockchain developers are working on quantum-resistant cryptography to future-proof blockchain networks.

Staying informed on quantum blockchain research and potentially running nodes that use quantum-resistant protocols could help you prepare for this next wave of technological development.

Artificial Intelligence (AI) and Blockchain:

The combination of blockchain and AI can lead to innovative solutions, especially in areas like data privacy, machine learning, and autonomous systems. Blockchain can ensure data integrity and privacy, while AI can provide insights from vast amounts of decentralized data.

By integrating AI algorithms with your blockchain node, you could help automate decision-making processes, optimize blockchain operations, or even develop decentralized AI-driven applications.

As blockchain technology continues to mature, so do the possibilities for its use in decentralized systems. By expanding your blockchain node setup and keeping an eye on emerging technologies, you can position yourself to take full advantage of the opportunities in decentralized finance, digital rights management, IoT, supply chains, and more. Blockchain is just the beginning, and as new developments continue to emerge, your role in the decentralized ecosystem can grow even more impactful.

Continuing to explore these new frontiers and integrating cutting-edge decentralized technologies into your node infrastructure will ensure that you're not only staying current but also contributing to the development of the decentralized world of tomorrow.

Appendices

Appendix A: Recommended Tools and Software

For anyone running or managing blockchain nodes, having the right tools and software is crucial to ensure efficiency, security, and optimal performance. Below is a list of essential tools and software to help blockchain node operators.

Blockchain Clients

Bitcoin Core
Link: https://bitcoincore.org
The official Bitcoin client for running a full node on the Bitcoin network. It allows you to download the entire Bitcoin blockchain and participate in the verification of transactions.

Geth (Go Ethereum)
Link: https://geth.ethereum.org
The most widely used client for running a full Ethereum node. Geth allows you to mine Ether, validate transactions, and interact with decentralized applications (dApps).

Litecoin Core
Link: https://litecoin.org
The official client for running a Litecoin full node. Litecoin is similar to Bitcoin but offers faster block generation times and different hashing algorithms.

Polkadot
Link: https://polkadot.network
A multi-chain blockchain framework for interoperability. Polkadot's node clients allow for the creation of specialized blockchain networks that communicate securely and efficiently with other blockchains.

Security Tools

Fail2ban
Link: https://www.fail2ban.org
A tool that helps protect your server from brute-force attacks by monitoring log files and blocking suspicious IP addresses.

UFW (Uncomplicated Firewall)
Link: https://help.ubuntu.com/community/UFW
A simple firewall management tool for Linux servers, which is particularly useful for configuring security rules for your blockchain node.

OpenSSH
Link: https://www.openssh.com
Essential for securely accessing your blockchain node remotely via SSH, ensuring encrypted communication between your server and client.

Monitoring Tools

Prometheus
Link: https://prometheus.io
A monitoring system and time-series database that is highly effective for tracking blockchain node performance, uptime, and transaction metrics.

Grafana
Link: https://grafana.com
An open-source analytics and monitoring platform that integrates with Prometheus for visualizing your blockchain node data and health metrics in real-time.

Netdata
Link: https://www.netdata.cloud
A monitoring tool for real-time metrics, focusing on server health and performance, including CPU, memory, disk I/O, and network statistics.

Appendix B: Troubleshooting Guide

Running blockchain nodes comes with its fair share of technical challenges. Below is a quick reference guide for resolving some common issues that blockchain node operators may encounter.

Common Blockchain Node Errors and Solutions

Error: Node not syncing with the blockchain.
Solution:

Ensure that your server has sufficient resources (e.g., memory, storage, and bandwidth) to handle blockchain syncing.

Check the node's logs for any network or database issues. Logs are typically found in the ~/.bitcoin/debug.log or ~/.ethereum/geth.log files.

Make sure your firewall or any security tools are not blocking incoming connections to your node's port (e.g., 8333 for Bitcoin or 30303 for Ethereum).

Error: Blockchain client crashes or freezes.
Solution:

Ensure your blockchain client is up to date. Older versions may have bugs that are fixed in newer releases.

If using Geth, try restarting it with the --syncmode light option to use a lighter, faster synchronization mode.

Check your disk space. Full nodes require significant storage, and running out of disk space can cause client crashes.

Error: Slow transaction propagation.
Solution:

Verify that your node is well-connected to other peers in the network. You can manually add peer nodes if necessary.

Consider adjusting the maxconnections parameter in the configuration to increase the number of outbound connections.

Check if your internet connection is stable and fast enough to support your node's communication with the blockchain network.

Error: Incorrect or outdated blockchain data.
Solution:

Delete the blockchain and chainstate folders and restart the node to force it to re-sync the blockchain from scratch.

Consider pruning old blocks with the prune=1 option in the configuration file to save disk space and ensure that only the latest data is retained.

Appendix C: Glossary of Blockchain Terms

Understanding blockchain terminology is essential for navigating the world of decentralized technologies.

Here are some key terms and concepts related to blockchain and cryptocurrency:

Blockchain: A decentralized, distributed ledger technology that records transactions across a network of computers in a secure, transparent, and immutable manner.

Node: A computer that participates in the blockchain network, maintaining a copy of the blockchain, validating transactions, and contributing to network consensus.

Full Node: A node that downloads the entire blockchain and verifies all transactions independently.

Miner: A node that participates in the proof-of-work consensus mechanism by solving cryptographic puzzles to add new blocks to the blockchain.

Validator: A node that participates in proof-of-stake or other consensus mechanisms to validate transactions and secure the network.

Proof of Work (PoW): A consensus algorithm used by Bitcoin and others, where miners solve complex mathematical problems to validate transactions and add blocks to the blockchain.

Proof of Stake (PoS): An alternative consensus algorithm where validators are chosen to create new blocks based on the number of coins they hold and are willing to "stake" as collateral.

Smart Contracts: Self-executing contracts where the terms of the agreement are written into code on the blockchain, automatically executing when conditions are met.

Wallet: A digital tool for storing and managing cryptocurrency, typically with a private key for accessing the blockchain.

Hashing: The process of transforming data into a fixed-size string of characters, typically using a cryptographic function, ensuring data integrity.

Token: A unit of value issued on top of a blockchain, typically used in decentralized applications, often representing assets, rights, or utilities.

Decentralized Finance (DeFi): A blockchain-based form of finance that operates without intermediaries, allowing users to borrow, lend, trade, and invest directly through smart contracts.

Appendix D: Resources for Further Learning

To continue expanding your knowledge about blockchain and Linux server administration, here are some valuable resources:

Blockchain Learning Resources

Bitcoin Whitepaper: The original whitepaper by Satoshi Nakamoto, detailing how Bitcoin works.

Mastering Bitcoin: A comprehensive guide to understanding Bitcoin, its architecture, and its operation.
Link: https://github.com/bitcoinbook/bitcoinbook

Ethereum Documentation: Official resources for learning how to develop on the Ethereum network.

Blockchain at Berkeley: Educational content and resources from the University of California, Berkeley, focused on blockchain development and research.

Linux Server Administration

DigitalOcean Community Tutorials: A wealth of tutorials on Linux server management, including security, performance optimization, and application hosting.

Linux Foundation Training: Professional training and certification for Linux system administration.
Link: https://www.linuxfoundation.org/

Communities and Forums

BitcoinTalk: A community forum for discussing Bitcoin, cryptocurrencies, and blockchain-related topics.
https://bitcointalk.org/

Ethereum StackExchange: A Q&A forum for Ethereum developers and users.
https://ethereum.stackexchange.com/

r/Blockchain: A subreddit dedicated to blockchain discussions, news, and resources.
https://www.reddit.com/r/Blockchain/

Stack Overflow: A popular platform where developers can ask questions and find answers related to blockchain development and programming.
https://stackoverflow.com/

Appendix E: Diverse List of Popular Blockchain Sites

Bitcoin (BTC)

The original cryptocurrency, Bitcoin operates on a decentralized blockchain and serves as a store of value and medium of exchange.
Website: https://bitcoin.org

Ethereum (ETH)

A blockchain platform for building decentralized applications (dApps) and executing smart contracts. Ethereum is the backbone for many DeFi projects and NFTs.
Website: https://ethereum.org

Audius
A decentralized music streaming platform that allows artists to directly upload and monetize their music, bypassing intermediaries like record labels and streaming services.
Website: https://audius.co

Livepeer
A decentralized video streaming platform that uses blockchain for video encoding, making streaming services more cost-effective and accessible.
Website: https://www.livepeer.org

Filecoin

A decentralized storage network that allows users to store and share files. Users can rent out their storage space and earn Filecoin tokens.
Website: https://filecoin.io

Axie Infinity

A blockchain-based game where players can buy, sell, and breed digital pets called Axies, earning cryptocurrency through gameplay. It's one of the most popular blockchain games.
Website: https://axieinfinity.com

OpenSea

The largest NFT marketplace, OpenSea allows users to buy, sell, and trade non-fungible tokens, including art, music, and virtual goods.
Website: https://opensea.io

Polkadot

A multi-chain network designed for interoperability between different blockchains, allowing decentralized applications to interact across chains securely.
Website: https://polkadot.network

Chainlink

A decentralized oracle network that connects smart contracts with real-world data, enabling dApps to interact with external systems like APIs and payment networks.
Website: https://chain.link

Tezos

A self-amending blockchain that supports smart contracts and decentralized applications, focused on governance, security, and scalability.
Website: https://tezos.com

Uniswap

A decentralized exchange (DEX) on Ethereum that allows users to trade cryptocurrencies directly from their wallets, bypassing centralized intermediaries.
Website: https://uniswap.org

Brave

A privacy-focused browser built on blockchain technology that rewards users with Basic Attention Token (BAT) for viewing ads and engaging with content.
Website: https://brave.com

MakerDAO

A decentralized autonomous organization that governs the Dai stablecoin, allowing users to access decentralized lending and borrowing services.
Website: https://makerdao.com

Sia

A decentralized storage platform that allows users to rent out unused hard drive space, ensuring data privacy and reliability through blockchain technology.
Website: https://sia.tech

Celo

A mobile-first blockchain designed to make decentralized finance (DeFi) accessible to anyone with a smartphone, particularly in emerging markets.
Website: https://celo.org

Decentraland

A virtual world platform built on the Ethereum blockchain, where users can buy, sell, and build on digital land using the native MANA cryptocurrency.
Website: https://decentraland.org

Algorand

A scalable and secure blockchain platform designed for decentralized applications and digital assets, with a focus on speed and sustainability.
Website: https://algorand.com

VeChain

A blockchain platform designed for supply chain and logistics management, providing transparent and efficient solutions for tracking products and ensuring authenticity.
Website: https://www.vechain.org

Rarible

A decentralized NFT marketplace that allows creators to mint, buy, and sell digital collectibles, offering users full control over their assets.

Website: https://rarible.com

WAX

A blockchain designed for the creation, buying, and selling of virtual items and collectibles, with a focus on gaming and NFTs.

Website: https://wax.io

www.ingramcontent.com/pod-product-compliance
Lightning Source LLC
LaVergne TN
LVHW022347060326
832902LV00022B/4303